P9-DNE-645

TRANSFORMING
TRAUMA: EMDR®

TRANSFORMING
TRAUMA:EMDR®

The Revolutionary New Therapy
for Freeing the Mind, Clearing the
Body, and Opening the Heart

LAUREL PARNELL, PH.D.

W. W. NORTON & COMPANY   New York • London

For information about permission to reproduce selections from this book, write to
Permissions, W. W. Norton & Company, Inc., 500 Fifth Avenue, New York, NY 10110.

The text of this book is composed in Walbaum with display set in Charlemagne and Diotima. Composition and manufacturing by the Haddon Craftsmen, Inc. Book design by Charlotte Staub.

Library of Congress Cataloging-in-Publication Data

Parnell, Laurel, 1955–
    Transforming trauma—EMDR : the revolutionary new therapy for freeing the mind, clearing the body, and opening the heart / Laurel Parnell.
        p.   cm.
    Includes index.
    ISBN 0-393-04053-4
    1. Eye movement desensitization and reprocessing.   2. Psychic trauma—Treatment.   I. Title.
    RC489.E98P37   1997
    616.85'2106—dc21   96-44478   CIP

W. W. Norton & Company, Inc., 500 Fifth Avenue, New York, N.Y. 10110
http://www.wwnorton.com
W. W. Norton & Company, Ltd., 10 Coptic Street, London WC1A 1PU

1   2   3   4   5   6   7   8   9   0

To JEAN KLEIN

CONTENTS

ACKNOWLEDGMENTS

L ike the weaving of a tapestry, many different threads went into the creation of this book. I want to extend my heart-felt appreciation to all the wonderful people who helped make this book possible.

First of all I want to thank Francine Shapiro, whose broad vision, intelligence, compassion, and courage has made EMDR® the powerful life-changing therapy that it is.

Many people have insights, but few have the courage and compassion to actualize them as she has. Her support of this project has been greatly appreciated. I also wish to thank Robbie Dunton without whose dedication to the development of EMDR® and the EMDR® Institute none of this would be happening, and, A. J. Popky, whose steady, caring support of EMDR® from its inception has been so essential to its growth.

I thank all of the clients whose stories have been included in this book. They have been courageous in trying this new therapy and in their willingness to face their pain directly. Their emerging renewed taught me much about the power of EMDR® and deeply moved and inspired me.

Thanks to all of my fellow EMDR® facilitators from whom I have learned so much during the years. I especially want to thank Linda Cohn, friend and colleague, whose insights into working with clients who have been sexually abused were very valuable.

Thank you too to EMDR® therapists and facilitators Craig Penner, Robert Oxlade, Leilani Lewis, and Brooke Passano, whose support of this project was very appreciated.

I want to thank all those who were helpful in the birth and development of this book: C. J. Hayden for her wise guidance; Sheryl Fullerton, my agent who was invaluable in teaching and guiding me through this process; Ann Weinberger, who helped develop and edit the proposal; Brooke Brown, a terrific editor and friend who understood the essence of what I was trying to convey and was able to prune gently and yet keep the integrity of the writing; Margaret Allen, dear friend through thick and thin who was so supportive throughout the process and gave very helpful feedback; Richard Miller and John Prendergast, my friends and colleagues who supported me throughout the unfolding of this marvelous process; Jean Pumphrey, aunt, friend, mentor, whose lifelong support of my creative development will always be deeply appreciated; Alonnsi Ruvinski, dear friend, whose final editing and feedback were so timely and helpful; and, Susan Munro, editor at Norton, who saw the value in this book from the beginning and has supported its vision.

I want to thank my mother and stepfather, Helen and Bruce McDonald, for their enthusiastic support; and my father, Dean Parnell, for allowing our relationship to grow beyond the old patterns. My love and appreciation to my sons Catono and Etienne. Thank you, thank you, thank you to my beloved husband, Pierre-Antoine Blais, for his radiant love, wisdom, and support.

Finally, I want to extend my deepest, heartfelt gratitude to my two teachers, Lama Thubten Yeshe and Jean Klein.

PREFACE

This book was born out of my desire to share with others the "miracles" I have been privileged to witness both as a psychologist working with clients in a private practice setting and as an EMDR® Institute facilitator helping to train clinicians—as well as a recipient of EMDR® (eye movement desensitization and reprocessing) therapy. Many of my clients have exclaimed, "This is amazing!" during and/or after EMDR® processing sessions when they have had profound insights or cleared problems from their systems that had plagued them for most of their lives. I was compelled to take their stories into the world so that others might benefit.

During the last five years of doing EMDR® therapy, belief after belief of mine about what is possible to heal has shattered. I have found EMDR® helpful to a wide range of clients—from clients haunted by terrible abuse histories to fearful and/or rageful clients who had not found relief in other therapies. Repeatedly, I am awed by the transformative power of this therapy. I am no longer frustrated by what I had felt were limitations in my ability to help people. I am enthusiastic and optimistic about the work in a new way and no longer experience feeling burnt out. Rather, instead of feeling upset and disturbed at the end of EMDR® processing sessions full of clearing unspeakable horrors from childhood abuse, accidents, tragic losses, and violence, I feel *inspired and elated.* And, I am *not* alone in these feelings. Every EMDR® therapist with whom I've spoken who uses this method extensively in his or her practice shares my enthusiasm. EMDR® conferences are oases of celebration and the sharing of successes.

There are also many effects of EMDR® therapy that have not been written about which are very common and distinguish it from other therapies. EMDR® therapy takes us *beyond* recovery from trauma to a sense of joy, openness, and deep connection with ourselves and our lives. With EMDR® we seem to be experiencing a quantum leap in our ability to heal trauma and maladaptive beliefs and behaviors.

EMDR® has also been taken out of the confines of psychotherapy offices and used to help victims of large-scale human disasters. Early on, EMDR® clinicians offered assistance in a variety of settings. For example, following the devastation of Hurricane Andrew in Florida, the 1994 Northridge earthquake in Southern California, and the bombing in Oklahoma City, groups of EMDR® clinicians responded by offering free services to survivors. EMDR® trainers and facilitators went to Oklahoma City and volunteered their time to train more than three hundred local clinicians so that they would have the tools necessary to continue the healing that would be needed in the future.

The EMDR® Humanitarian Assistance Program (EMDR®-HAP) was formed to bring EMDR® wherever it is needed throughout the world. Pro bono trainings have been given in Croatia, Bosnia, Columbia, the Ukraine, Israel, and

Nairobi for clinicians working with Rwandan refugee children. As of this writing, trainings are planned in Yugoslavia, Hungary, El Salvador, Guatemala, Northern Ireland, and the Navajo Nation. EMDR®-HAP aims to provide EMDR®-centered psychological services at low or no cost to violence and disaster victims and their care providers and to assist local mental health professionals in meeting the long-term emotional needs of traumatic stress survivors in their own communities by training them in EMDR® and to encourage research, development, and implementation of EMDR®-centered psychological programs designed to reduce all forms of traumatic stress.

EMDR® therapy has applications for many different problems, and the types of applications are expanding constantly. At a recent EMDR® international conference, I was moved repeatedly by therapists' inspiring stories of healing. These stories included:

• The cancer-stricken Colombian girl who had just had her leg amputated and was hysterical with phantom limb pain. The staff at the group home where she resided were unable to alleviate her distress. After a few EMDR® processing sessions by a volunteer EMDR® clinician, the pain disappeared and the girl began to fantasize a future that included playing with other children.

• The Philadelphia railroad engineer who, despite witnessing several people's deaths on the train tracks during the years, continued to function until he witnessed the suicide of an eight-month pregnant woman who used his train to end her life. EMDR® therapy helped to clear the horrifying image of her looking into his eyes before she was killed as well as his nightmares. Inspired and grateful, he has be-

come an active advocate of EMDR® to help other traumatized railroad engineers.

- The cool, sophisticated fifty-five-year-old socialite stricken
  with terminal cancer who had always lived behind a self-
  created barrier to intimacy with her friends and family
  members. Stoically, she underwent chemotherapy and ra-
  diation treatments alone, never sharing her pain or suffering. After several EMDR® processing sessions she was able
  to lower the barrier and connect openly with friends and
  family—for the first time—before she died. In a voice
  weakened by the ravages of the disease, a few days before
  her death she told her EMDR® therapist, "I am a different
  person now. Thank you."

All of the stories in this book are true although identifying information has been changed to protect confidentiality.
Some of the clients are composites, and nearly all of the cases
described were from my private psychotherapy practice.

EMDR® is a comprehensive, integrative therapy which is
taught only to licensed mental health professionals or mental
health interns who are supervised by licensed clinicians
trained in EMDR®. As you will see later in the book, EMDR®
is a very powerful method which can open people to previously
unknown images and intense emotional experiences. Therefore, it is important that non-therapists and therapists not for-
mally trained in EMDR® not attempt to use the eye
movements on themselves or others. It is not this book's intention to teach the EMDR® protocol and procedure; rather,
I want to introduce you to this transformational new therapy.

In this book I share stories of healing that demonstrate
some of the unusual effects EMDR® has on trauma recovery.

I hope to inspire you to go beyond the bounds of what you believe possible in healing and to be open to something new that has the potential to clear the past traumatic, life-limiting events from your body and mind, thus freeing you to live life to its fullest potential. It is my hope that this book will open your mind and heart to the vast possibilities of healing ourselves and our world.

TRANSFORMING
TRAUMA: EMDR®

CHAPTER 1

How EMDR® Changed My Life

MY INTRODUCTION TO EYE MOVEMENT DESENSITIZATION AND REPROCESSING (EMDR®)

It was a warm spring day in the vast California desert, resplendent with brilliantly flowering cactuses and wild flowers. Inside the large meditation hall, a group of about one hundred yoga students, clad in light-colored yoga clothes, silently and slowly followed the instructions of the teacher, Jean Klein. Moving with mindfulness, allowing each posture to unfold in stillness, we moved in a fluid meditation.

Suddenly, the silence in the room was interrupted by the sound of heavy breathing and a thud, thud, thud! My meditation disturbed, I looked out of the corner of my eye and saw one of the yoga students removing his clothes and doing jumping jacks and calisthenics. As he was jumping up and down, he was emitting strange sounds and seemed oblivious to those around him. Dressed only in his underwear, he was sweating profusely and was quite agitated. This behavior continued throughout the two-hour yoga session. It was obvious to many of us who were psychotherapists at this seminar that he was experiencing some kind of manic or psychotic episode.

At lunch that day with my friends Richard and Garnita, both psychologists from the San Francisco Bay Area, we shared what was new in our personal and professional lives. Garnita, who was an experienced therapist and clinical supervisor, told us that she had learned a new therapeutic method that used eye movements to clear what she referred to as "psychological memory." This method had totally changed her psychotherapy practice, and she was getting excellent results with all kinds of different clients and problems. I was skeptical, however, and not very interested in fad techniques, but I respected Garnita and her work. As she described the method, I thought it very strange and the results too good to be true. Our conversation moved to the yoga student who had acted bizarrely that morning. Believing EMDR® would help him, Garnita decided to speak with him and offer to work with him intensively.

The next morning at yoga, I noticed that the formerly agitated and bizarrely behaving yoga student was properly dressed and silently doing the yoga postures with the group. He went through the two-hour yoga/meditation session without any outward signs of disturbance. Curious, I asked Richard what had changed the student? Had he taken some kind of tranquilizer? Richard told me that Garnita had spent an intensive period of time using EMDR® with him, which had settled him. I was amazed. Furthermore, this man remained calm and appropriate throughout the rest of the seminar. Intrigued by this result and impressed by Garnita's enthusiasm for this method, I signed up for the next EMDR® training, which was to be given in three weeks.

The EMDR® Training

The EMDR® training was held in a large hotel ballroom in Sunnyvale, California. About sixty of us, all licensed psychotherapists sitting with yellow pads in our laps, listened attentively to Francine Shapiro, the originator of EMDR®, explain the theory and research. As Dr. Shapiro strode steadily back and forth, microphone in hand, she interwove theories of "neuro networks" and "adaptive information processing" with moving stories of healing from trauma. She exhibited a strong and compassionate presence, keen intelligence, quick wit, and self-assurance. I immediately felt the quality and integrity of what was being presented. Not trained as a cognitive-behaviorist, much of the language and vocabulary used was new to me, and I felt challenged to expand my knowledge. I learned that EMDR® is a comprehensive treatment with many components—it is much more than simply eye movements. There are also many different protocols, and it is imperative that the appropriate protocol be used. For instance, the protocol for childhood sexual abuse treatment differs from that for treatment for a recent traumatic incident.

After several hours of lecture interspersed with video case examples, we were ready to practice the EMDR® procedure. We divided into trios; one person acted as therapist, another as client, and the third as observer. Trained EMDR® facilitators answered any questions and aided the therapists in the procedure. We were told to select a memory that wasn't very disturbing to us, that was a five on a scale of zero to ten. I chose a childhood memory that didn't feel particularly charged to me but that I remembered well. I was in fifth grade, and the teacher from the other fifth-grade class summoned me into his classroom while his class was in session. I remembered him as tall, with dark hair, baggy pants, and a mustache. And, although I didn't know why, I felt he didn't like me. On this particular day I thought he was calling me into his class to give me some good news. Many of the members of the choir were to be selected to sing in a Peanuts cartoon special, and I was hoping that I was going to be chosen. When I got into his class, I felt very self-conscious. He beckoned me to the front of the class. There, towering over me, he angrily accused me of spreading rumors about the TV show and told me that I would not be chosen. I was stunned and had no idea what he was talking about. Totally hurt and humiliated, I began to cry.

We started with the most disturbing *image*—that of the angry teacher towering over me and denouncing me. The *feeling* was of being stunned, humiliated, and frightened. The *belief* associated with the memory was "I am powerless." The therapist asked me to hold these three components—image, feeling, and belief—together in my mind and to follow her fingers with my eyes. What happened next was very surprising to me. She moved her fingers across my field of vision, and I moved my eyes back and forth keeping my head steady. I experienced a range of very intense emotions. It was as if layers of an onion were peeling away one by one with each layer's removal revealing yet another layer. The first layer was the acute feeling of powerlessness and humiliation. The eye movements intensified the experience, moving it out of the realm of intellect and connecting me more fully to my emotions. When that feeling subsided, the therapist instructed me to "let it go" and take a deep breath. "What's happening now?" she asked. I felt very small and helpless. She told me to "go with that" and follow her fingers again.

Next I experienced a strong longing to be liked by the teacher and the hurt and betrayal of being so strongly disliked by him. I felt the hurt deep in my heart, and tears flowed from my eyes. I was surprised! I hadn't remembered that part before, but I knew it was true. I also was surprised by the power of my emotions. *Now* I was in unknown territory.

Things intensified. Quickly, another extremely disturbing childhood image—a ten on the scale—replaced the picture of that teacher. Shapiro had explained this phenomenon (image replacement) to us in her lecture earlier. The eye movements were causing associated memory networks to link and, in an accelerated fashion, I was processing my old memories. I was so disturbed by the memory of the teacher because it was linked to an earlier, emotionally charged memory of my father. In previous therapies I had examined my childhood and had seen an angry, distant father and a mother who felt caught in her role as homemaker. I had always believed they had done their best; however, my intellectual understanding had not permeated the beliefs or feelings that were fixed in my body and brain.

In the earlier memory, I was two or three years old and in the bathroom. My pants were down around my ankles and I was trying to clean myself after wetting my pants. My father was towering over me and I perceived homicidal rage in his dark eyes. There I was, defenseless and vulnerable, and he had found me.

Although this was not a new memory and I had been able to relate it without emotion on earlier occasions, during the practicum exercise I fully reexperienced my absolute terror and vulnerability. My perception shifted radically. *I was a small child again, and he looked like a giant.* I was experiencing this memory from the child's point of view. When I had related this memory previously to psychotherapists, I had been an adult recounting an experience from the past. Now, I *was* the child. Simultaneously, I witnessed the experience as if I were watching a movie. My adult self was the aware witness; consciously, I identified with the child.

As I followed the therapist's fingers, the most unspeakable terror filled me. Heat flashed throughout my body and my breath peaked and dipped rapidly high in my chest. I felt out of control of my body. The child was convinced that her father was going to kill her. The therapist's fingers kept moving and I continued to move my eyes back and forth. There was something very soothing about the steady movement and connection with this caring guide, who occasionally encouraged me by saying, "good," "it's old stuff," and "just let it go." After a surge of intensity the feeling would subside and the therapist would say, "Close your eyes, take a deep breath, and let it go." Then I would pause, tell her what I had experienced, and describe my present state.

In the next round of eye movements I experienced my father asking me if I had wet my pants. I was trapped. I knew that if I told the truth, "I'd get it." Also, if I lied, "I'd get it." I thought of George Washington and the cherry tree—but I lied. Then, my father called me a liar and began to spank me. My terror was overwhelming. I breathed rapidly, my body shook, I felt dizzy, and I began to black out. The *child* believed that he was going to kill her.

After a few minutes of processing, I felt calmer. I closed my eyes and reported my experience to the therapist. Speaking, I realized that as a child I felt that there was no one to help me, no one to protect me. The *child's* reality was that my mother did nothing to stop my father from hurting me on this or any other occasion. Following my therapist's instruction to "go with that," I saw how my child self felt that my mother had never protected me from my father. I experienced how my child self felt totally alone and unprotected and I was angry at my mother for not protecting me. I pictured her in front of me and told her that it was her job to protect the little girl from the angry father. Then, doubt that my mother had loved me came into my child's mind—doubt because I never felt protected.

I recognized a core belief—one that had affected my interpersonal relationships. I did not believe that I could trust anyone to be there for me. I had to take care of myself. I could count on myself—but no one else. I always prided myself on being independent, but now I saw that my independence derived from my belief that I could not trust my parents to love and protect me.

As the eye movements continued, I felt a profound sense of betrayal. I realized I had lost trust in others. I saw that there'd been a time when I did trust, but I had decided never to trust again. Tremendous grief flooded through me and I sobbed and sobbed. Yet, out of the grief came a feeling of deep love. Even though I didn't believe others could love me, I knew I loved myself. The little girl had done her best and I completely loved her. Spontaneously, I desired to hold and rock her in my arms and I imagined doing so as I continued to move my eyes back and forth.

Unfortunately, the session's allotted time elapsed before I could complete my work with this memory. So, the therapist made sure I was calm enough to end the session. We knew we could continue the next day.

That day I began my session with the memory of my father discovering me with my pants down in the bathroom. This time, my emotion was less intense than on the previous day. As I began the eye movements, I felt the rage I felt as a child at him for hurting and humiliating me. Thoughts followed—he had *no* right to treat me that way. Imaginatively, I surrounded myself with other people in my present life who would protect me and then my child self yelled at him and expressed all that I had needed to express. I did all of this while following the therapist's fingers. My anger passed, and I felt deep calm and relief.

Next, I felt rejected by him, and with this I felt a great deal of sadness for I had *so* wanted him to love me. My heart opened to my child self who had felt unloved and unwanted. With the next set of eye movements I experienced wanting my father's love—for, indeed, I did love him very much. By the session's end I felt compassion for myself and for my father. My heart was quite open and I felt cleansed.

These initial EMDR® sessions taught me many things. For one, I learned firsthand that the child can perceive something to be mortally dangerous and have that initial perception become locked in its original form in the body-mind. (What happens to the body affects the mind, and vice versa. For that reason I often use the term "body-mind" when discussing the effects of trauma.) Just because the child believed her father was going to kill her or could potentially kill her did not mean *he* had those intentions. I really understood that my child's experience was frozen in time with the thoughts, feelings, and beliefs as they had been thirty-three years earlier. I understood that it isn't what happened that is imprinted, but rather *what one perceives to have happened.* These sessions helped me to understand why I had never processed this information although I had spent four years in Jungian analysis and two years of psychodynamic psychotherapy. It was simply too much to reexperience. However, EMDR® allowed the information to be experienced at an *accelerated* rate. I did not remain stuck in any of the intense states for long. Rather, I moved through them as if swimming through waves that would build up, peak, and then subside. After awhile I was confident that I could ride those waves and that the intense emotions would pass.

One of the most amazing outcomes of these initial personal EMDR® sessions was learning that not only could I go into and process intensely painful emotions, but that I could also feel love, compassion, and understanding for those whom I had perceived to have harmed me. During those sessions I gained many insights as to the origins of many of my lifelong patterns, particularly around the issues of trust, betrayal, fear, vulnerability, and the belief that no one but myself could love me; I noted these matters to work on in future sessions. Unquestionably, I felt a deep respect and regard for EMDR® and the power it held for healing.

After the workshop and these very powerful EMDR® sessions, I had planned to go to my father's house for his sixtieth birthday party. Exhausted and exhilarated after the workshop, I was profoundly moved by what I had learned and experienced. I was inspired by EMDR®'s potential for healing myself and my clients, and this meeting with my father would test the immediate effects of the workshop sessions. I had not seen my father for about five years because of a falling out we had, the origins of which came from these early childhood events, but we had begun to reconnect after he suffered a significant loss in his life and I phoned to offer him support.

He greeted me warmly as I walked into his house. This was not the angry, young father of my childhood. Instead, I saw a handsome, gray-haired, sixty-year-old man who was beaming with happiness, and I was struck immediately by how much I loved and cared about him. My fear and tension which had always been in the background were gone. Despite feeling very open and vulnerable after the EMDR® session, I felt much more at ease with him. In the past, because of my underlying fear and anger, I had always related to him on an intellectual level, thus keeping him at a friendly but safe distance. On this occasion, as well as subsequent interactions since the EMDR® work, my anger and fear were gone. I have felt much more comfortable and at ease around him. This isn't something I think about or try to do—it just is different now when I think about it. The old way of relating no longer exists.

My fear and anger peeled off, exposing a layer of longing. At the time of the party, I felt hurt at not feeling loved by him; I was aware of the little girl wanting her daddy to love her. I was close to tears as I felt this longing that I had always denied because I didn't believe his love existed for me. But, suppressing my longing caused other problems for me. I do need to be loved.

I enjoyed the party and the birth of a new relationship with my father. I felt closer and more connected to him. Without the baggage from the past, I was less burdened and was clearer.

These EMDR® sessions profoundly impacted my life. Many of the insights and issues that arose provided areas for more

work. The layer of hurt along with the belief that I couldn't
be loved by a man screamed for attention at the forefront of
my awareness. These beliefs had caused me great pain in most
of my adult relationships with men. So, I began to see an
EMDR® therapist to work specifically on these issues.

The End of an Unhappy Marriage

Things in my marriage were not going well. Although my
husband and I cared deeply about one another, we were fun-
damentally incompatible as mates and had struggled for years
to make our marriage work. We rode a roller coaster through
times of closeness tailed by times of wrenching incompati-
bility. Neither of us wanted to give up despite our great difficulties. We felt that because of our marriage vows and many
common interests we should keep the marriage intact despite
our suffering and frustration.

During an EMDR® processing session I focused on the un-
happiness I felt in our marriage and felt a strong pain in my
heart and tension throughout my body. Beginning with these
physical sensations, my eyes followed the therapist's fingers
moving back and forth horizontally and allowed my painful
thoughts and emotions to unfold. In this life-changing session
I processed an entire range of feelings about myself and my
husband and realized in a deeper, more integrated way how
unhappy I was. I realized that the marriage truly was not
working for either of us and saw that I was clutching onto an
ideal of marriage that I could not attain. I realized that the
marriage was over: we had outgrown the form and needed to
shed it as a crab sheds its shell in order to grow. The form of

marriage and our ideals kept us from growing emotionally and spiritually. All of this information came to me spontaneously, seemingly out of nowhere as things do in EMDR® sessions, and felt completely true.

A deep sense of relief and an enormous flood of energy rushed through my body with my realization that the marriage was finished, and a blissful feeling of joy and freedom came in its wake. I felt certain that my husband would agree with my understanding and that we would both be able to honor our past and step out of the constraints of the marriage.

In the days following this EMDR® session I felt a constant inner processing and a need to write. Time felt accelerated, speeded up with many new insights. The form of marriage no longer supported us: we had done all we could do together. I felt love and appreciation for my husband and gratitude for all he had given me in our life together. All the while, I continued to feel a tremendous sense of relief at the resolution I was experiencing. I felt a sense of deep forgiveness and compassion for both of us; I had not erred in marrying him for that was exactly what I had to do at that time. We had grown a great deal in our open and honest relationship.

I shared my realizations with him, and he agreed that we should end the marriage. We had both tried so very hard to make our marriage work, but the truth was that we were both deeply unhappy. I grieved as I remembered the good times we had shared, but my grief lasted only for a short time before the joy and feeling of freedom returned. The EMDR® session had accelerated the end of our dying marriage and, finally, I was able to cease struggling.

I continued to process the marriage in my next few EMDR®

sessions and felt as if I were cleansing my heart of blockage which had prevented me from feeling fully alive; EMDR® therapy helped me to feel more connected to myself. Many feelings regarding the ending of the marriage coursed through me as I used the eye movements: fear of the unknown, grief and loss, and excitement in anticipation of a new life. As I completed these sessions I also affirmed what I wanted in my life and felt increasingly free and spacious in my body and mind. I felt physically lighter.

I believe that EMDR® greatly helped me end my marriage in a healthy and clear way. Although the ending was painful, I believe the EMDR® sessions accelerated the processing of the painful feelings so that I could move through them quickly. Throughout the entire dissolution of the marriage I felt connected to a deep part of myself that I could trust; the EMDR® sessions maintained this body-based connection. This trust sustained me because often my emerging uncensored thoughts and feelings represented truth that I had not admitted to myself or anyone else.

CLEARING THE OBSTACLES TO A HEALTHY AND FULFILLING RELATIONSHIP

I met the love of my life at another yoga/meditation seminar I attended a year after I had been introduced to EMDR® by my friend Garnita. Happy and free, thanks to my EMDR® work and decision to end my marriage, I was feeling more and more myself again. I enjoyed my autonomy and had no desire to enter another relationship in the near future. It was wonderful at this seminar: I loved being in the desert with my friends, doing the beautiful yoga postures, and listening in the afternoons to the wise words of Jean Klein.

One night after meditation I met a wonderful man with whom I felt a very deep and immediate connection. His loving presence felt very familiar, and although most of our contact was in silence, I developed a profound love for him—I felt "home" when I was with him. At the end of the seminar we exchanged addresses and thought we might get together sometime but did not set a time.

Two weeks later he contacted me, and we spent a few days together, greatly enjoying each other. Although I did not know him well, I felt *so* much love for him. He lived quite far away, and when he left me I felt very sad, not knowing when I'd see him again. However, he indicated he would keep in touch.

Even though neither of us was ready for a committed relationship, during the next month I heard little from him and felt terribly hurt and rejected, an experience that stimulated the issues of rejection I had felt from my father. In my EMDR® therapy I concentrated on these feelings of rejection and accessed a deep pool of pain from feeling unloved and unwanted. The eye movements enabled me to let this pain pass through me, and tears flowed down my cheeks as a kind of purification as I released it.

As I released my pain, I became aware of core beliefs about myself that had limited my life and relationships. These beliefs stemmed from my believing that I was somehow flawed and to blame for the lack of love. "Why couldn't my father love me? What was wrong with me?" I wondered as I moved my eyes back and forth.

I felt that there was something essential lacking in me that caused my father to reject me. Simultaneously, I realized the fallacy of these feelings. Just putting into words what I had been feeling below my conscious awareness created space around the feelings. I disidentified from those feelings: I no longer felt I was lacking—rather, I could observe that I had erroneously attributed the cause of his anger to myself.

Soon another insight dawned. I was aware that I didn't believe it was possible for me to get love and attention. As a child I had experienced the futility of wanting my father's love and, consequently, I stopped wanting it for in that way I could avoid hurting. I realized that I did the same thing as an adult. To avoid inevitable pain and disappointment I stopped wanting things from my partners. I denied my deepest needs in relationships and settled for less than what I truly wanted.

Doing the eye movements, I stated affirmatively what I wanted in relationships. "I want to be loved and treated like I'm special and important—as if I matter. I want to be wanted by my partner. I want to want a man who then wants me rather than to want a man because he wants me." As I spoke, I strengthened. I *could* state my wants! I wouldn't necessarily get them, but I had a right to state them.

In one pivotal EMDR® session my therapist and I decided to work on traumatic childhood incidents in which I had felt physically threatened by my father. I began with the time described earlier when my father had found me with my pants down around my ankles. During the processing I discovered that I believed that I was to blame for all of his anger—that I had caused him to be an angry man. My adult self had known that my parents "had to get married" because my mother was pregnant with me, and I believed that my birth had ruined his life because he was stuck with a wife he hardly knew and with whom he was incompatible—and a baby he didn't want. Somehow it was my fault. I should never have been born; my conception and birth were a terrible mistake. Consequently, I felt terribly sad and depressed. In retrospect, I had always felt at fault for his anger, as do most children who have suffered at the hands of parents who are angry because of pain in their lives, but my reasoning came with the passage of time and with more information.

I was processing these feelings when suddenly I had an "Ah ha!" experience. It was as though I (my child self) was no longer in the center of the picture. I saw or sensed that my father's anger predated my birth, that his mother's mistreatment and neglect of him had much more to do with his anger than my birth. His anger wasn't about me; rather, I was but one part of a complex whole. This insight brought me a feeling of physical release, mental clarity, and peace. With the next round of eye movements I felt love for my father. Love and compassion for him had opened and filled my heart.

To close this session my therapist asked me to think about the men in my life who I felt loved me. I imagined the little girl in her grandfather's lap, his warm hands holding her. She felt very loved, protected, and wanted. Evoking this feeling and belief, I moved my eyes back and forth allowing them to integrate with the old image and belief that I could not be loved by a man. They couldn't both be true. Some men did love me and some did not. It had more to do with them than with me.

During the intensive EMDR® work I had become increasingly aware of other beliefs that had been running my life. I journaled daily between sessions and would bring the beliefs

I'd identified to the sessions. My inner processing was in high gear and I was constantly having insights—in the shower, when I was driving my car, standing in the check-out line at the market—it was as if any instant that opened was immediately filled with another insight. Everything in my life accelerated and intensified! My inner confidence grew with each EMDR® session, and I felt I could clear impediments to a full and joyful life; as any blockage in my mind or body appeared, I targeted it for future EMDR® sessions.

Two-and-a-half years after our meeting in the desert, the wonderful loving man and I were married in a beautiful ceremony surrounded by family and friends. Having lived together in a truly loving and harmonious relationship for two years, we believed that the actual marriage rite simply confirmed what had already happened. Before our wedding I had a dream in which I was with a group of people at a conference or party. A sickly, physically unattractive, needy man approached me and let me know that he wanted and needed me. Instantly, I recognized my old pattern: to respond to this man's needs rather than my own. However, in this dream I felt no compulsion to go with him. Instead, I informed him that I was already married to someone I loved very much.

This dream validated my transformation facilitated by the intensive EMDR® therapy. I felt loved. I knew what I wanted in a relationship. I no longer felt compelled to be with a man to whom I wasn't attracted simply because he desired me. Now I believed I could be with the man *I* wanted. I could love and be loved.

In my marriage I feel loved and cared for. A consistent flow of love and caring runs between us. Giving and receiving is

mutual. For the most part, old patterns are gone and our relationship does not resemble former ones in any manner. We
are both strong, happy people who enjoy life and one another.

My Work as an EMDR® Therapist and Teacher

My personal experiences as a client greatly inspired me to use
EMDR® with my clients. After completing the first EMDR®
training, I began using EMDR® with my clients and was impressed by the immediate positive results. I found that in several cases the introduction of EMDR® accelerated the therapy
process; clients moved through material and issues they had
been working on at a much faster pace after EMDR®, and
many clients completed therapy much sooner than they ordi-
narily would have.

Also, I found that in a relatively short time period I could
help clients who had suffered from early childhood traumas
such as sexual and physical abuse become free from the nightmares, flashbacks, and negative self-concepts. Furthermore,
we would clear the effects of the early abuse once and for all.
The memory could no longer emotionally disturb the client.

Several months later, I took the second level of training offered by the EMDR® Institute and went on to train as an
EMDR® facilitator so that I could help in the training of therapists. During the past several years I have been privileged to
witness and guide hundreds of clients and therapists/ trainees
in this life-changing therapy. So many people suffering from
the effects of traumas that have severely limited their lives
have come to see me; as a result of EMDR® therapy, they have

cleared the traumatic events from their systems. Clients have moved on with living their lives free from the old images, beliefs, and behaviors. EMDR® has also helped clients to open their hearts to compassion and love for themselves and others.

CHAPTER 2

What is EMDR® and How Does it Work?

As the devastating bombing of the federal building in Oklahoma City in 1995 began to fade from headline news, so did it dissipate from most people's minds. Yet for the thousands of residents whose lives it affected directly, the memory remained all too vivid.

Foreseeing the emotional havoc that threatened to overwhelm the city long after the disaster, the FBI came to the rescue by contacting the EMDR® Institute. With its worldwide recognition for success in treating trauma victims, EMDR® was the ideal solution for this emergency situation. A team of EMDR® therapists set up offices in Oklahoma City where therapists from throughout the country volunteered their services and treated more than two hundred survivors and their family members—as well as traumatized rescue workers and mental health providers.

To ensure continued treatment of the stricken population, volunteer EMDR® trainers and facilitators converged to train more than three hundred Oklahoma therapists, whose services would undoubtedly be sought by a large number of Oklahoma residents. I was part of the team that taught the advanced training and I will never forget hearing a grateful fireman at the closing ceremony of the training say in a voice choked with emotion, "It is because of EMDR® that I was able to go back to work."

EMDR® is more than a treatment entailing eye movements; it is a complex, multiphasic type of therapy that incorporates the eye movements into a comprehensive approach. EMDR® views dysfunctional behavior as originating from traumatic past incidents, which when skillfully identified can be targeted, processed, and integrated, resulting in adaptive and functional behaviors.

SHAPIRO'S DISCOVERY

It was only eight years before the EMDR® Institute was called upon by the federal government that the concept behind the therapy had been discovered—by accident, as many scientific breakthroughs are. On a spring day in 1987, Francine Shapiro, a graduate student in psychology, was walking through a park in Los Gatos, California. Disturbing thoughts that had been plaguing her suddenly began to disappear. When she retrieved them, she noticed they were distinctly less distressing. She was intrigued and began to closely monitor her thought processes. She noticed that when a disturbing thought came into her mind, her eyes began to move very rapidly. The eye movement seemed to cause the thought to shift out of her consciousness. When she recalled the thought, it had lost much of its negative charge. Then, she began doing this experiment deliberately, thinking about things—both past and present—that bothered her and moving her eyes rapidly. Each time the disturbance ceased. Curious to know if this discovery would work on other people, she tried it on her friends. By having them follow her finger with their eyes, she helped them to sustain their eye movements.

After testing this process on about seventy individuals, Shapiro realized that the eye movements had desensitized the individuals to their disturbing thoughts. She refined the process and named it eye movement desensitization (EMD), and in 1990 expanded the name to EMDR® to include the concept of processing. Further experience had convinced her that the eye movements also processed traumatic memories, making them more adaptive and functional. All along the way, Shapiro has developed her theory according to what she has observed.

In 1988 Shapiro tested her new method on twenty-two volunteers in an empirical study conducted in Mendocino, California. The subjects were either Vietnam vets or victims of rape or sexual abuse and all suffered from various symptoms of posttraumatic stress disorder (PTSD): nightmares, flashbacks, intrusive thoughts, low self-esteem, relationship problems, and persistent traumatic memories. After symptom assessment and measurement, the volunteers were divided randomly into two groups. Those in the first group were given an EMDR® session, while those in the second group were asked instead to give detailed descriptions of their traumatic experiences. After a single EMDR® procedure the treatment group had a significant reduction in symptoms. The non-EMDR® group showed virtually no changes. For ethical reasons the second group was then given an EMDR® session, which proved to decrease their symptoms as well. One and three months later the original treatment group was measured again; the positive results of their single EMDR® treatment had stayed with them.

In 1989 Shapiro's study was published in the *Journal of Traumatic Stress Studies*. Subsequently she met John Wolpe, a renowned behavioral therapist and theoretician, and told him about EMDR® and her research findings. Skeptical, he tried EMDR® with a few of his own clients. His trials were successful, and he agreed to publish her research findings in the *Journal of Behavioral Therapy and Experimental Psychiatry*. The next year Wolpe published his own case study of a severely traumatized rape victim who had not responded to traditional psychotherapy but experienced dramatic improvement after ten sessions of EMDR®. Wolpe's support gave EMDR® the legitimacy it needed to reach a wider audience.

Shapiro continued to present her findings to researchers at universities and Veterans' Administration centers across the country. In 1990, after publication of her dissertation and several influential journal articles, she offered the first EMDR® training seminar.

As word of this new trauma treatment spread throughout the academic and clinical communities, other researchers began to conduct studies on EMDR®. One of the most significant studies was done by EMDR®-trained researchers Sandra Wilson, Robert Tinker, and Lee Becker. A psychology graduate student from Colorado Springs, Wilson became interested in EMDR® when an enthusiastic colleague convinced her to go through the training. She later became so impressed with its power for healing PTSD that she made EMDR® the focus of her doctoral dissertation research.

Wilson's group of researchers sought to replicate the find-

ings of Shapiro's original study while improving the research
method by using several therapists and an independent as-
sessor to evaluate the results. They recruited forty men and
forty women with traumatic memories. All of the volunteers
were skeptical because no other therapy had helped them.
Since the time they experienced their traumas—from three
months to more than fifty years prior to the study—the volunteers had suffered from anxieties, phobias, sleep disturbances, intimacy problems, and depression. The men and
women were randomly assigned to either a treatment or
delayed-treatment group and to one of five EMDR® therapists.
After the members of the treatment group were given three
EMDR® sessions, their symptoms lessened markedly, both
immediately following the treatment and when tested three
months later. The untreated group showed no improvement.
However, when these delayed-treatment participants did receive their EMDR® sessions, they also experienced relief from
their symptoms. Another follow-up study was conducted fifteen months after the EMDR® therapy. Treatment benefits
had continued, and many of the volunteers said that they had
greater self-confidence and felt they could now deal with
whatever might happen in their lives.

Air Force Sergeant Dawn Baumgartner's compelling story
illustrates the study's results. While stationed in Panama the
year before the study, Dawn was awakened one night with a
knife to her throat. Two men had broken into her house, bur-
glarized it, and raped her while she was holding her five-year-
old daughter. The trauma of that horrific night caused Dawn
to experience uncontrollable crying, nightmares, insomnia,
flashbacks, and trouble concentrating on her work. Six months
of rape crisis counseling did little to alleviate her symptoms.

But, after her participation in the Wilson EMDR® study, Dawn was no longer overwhelmed by her memory of the rape. "It's okay now," she says. "It happened in my life, and now I can put it behind me and go on."

Eric Smith's story also attests to the success of EMDR® therapy. Smith, a Vietnam vet who was "severely depressed for over twenty years" after fighting in the war attests to EMDR®'s success. Eric was haunted by the feeling that he hadn't done enough during the war to keep fellow soldiers from getting killed. Although he had been in traditional therapy for years, he hadn't been able to get past his depression— once, he was inches away from jumping out of a sixth-floor hotel window. He sought help in a veterans' outreach program and found his way to Francine Shapiro seven years ago. To his delight, after one EMDR® processing session he felt better: "Two or three weeks later that stuff wouldn't come back." Eric continued with a few more EMDR® sessions and "resolved issues that I'd been discussing for four or five years with other people." He now runs his own research and development company in Santa Clara, California, is married, and has children. "Life couldn't be better," he says. "Everything, everything is wonderful."

THE NEW PROZAC OR THE OLD SNAKE OIL?

As evidence of EMDR®'s effectiveness mounted, there was a flurry of publicity in the mass media. Speculation abounded. *Newsweek* bluntly asked, "Is the trendy therapy technique called EMDR® the new Prozac or the old snake oil?" Criticism has also come from some academicians and clinicians who complain that EMDR® has been overpromoted, underresearched, and oversold. But the fact is that more controlled studies have been conducted on EMDR® than on any other method used to treat trauma and most studies have shown significant results.

Much of the resistance to EMDR® stems from the challenge it presents to clinicians' attitudes about therapy. Many believe that recovery from trauma is a lifelong process. Therapists may also be wedded to a particular school or approach to therapy and feel threatened by EMDR®'s effectiveness. But why should clients spend years and thousands of dollars lying on a couch when they could be enjoying life to the fullest?

The success rate of EMDR®, regardless of the resistance to it, speaks for itself. In a survey of EMDR®-trained clinicians who together had treated more than ten thousand clients, about 74 percent of the respondents reported EMDR® to be more effective than other treatments they had used, and only 3 percent found it less effective. The acceptance of EMDR® is also evident in the number of therapists who have been trained in its methodology since its discovery less than a decade ago. There are more than eighteen thousand EMDR®-trained psychotherapists worldwide who treat hundreds of thousands of clients. In addition to the training conducted by the EMDR® Institute, in 1995 universities and psychology graduate schools began offering EMDR® courses.

The growing body of EMDR® research and reports of its success in institutional settings also attest to its increasing acceptance as an effective therapy. EMDR® has become a routine treatment at more than a dozen Veterans' Administration centers across the country. According to Dr. Howard Lipke, former director of a treatment program for combat-related PTSD

at the Veterans' Hospital in North Chicago, EMDR® is "by far
the most effective therapeutic procedure we have." Of the
nearly two hundred Vietnam vets he has treated with
EMDR®, about 80 percent showed improvement. Lipke's results were corroborated by the findings of a study with Vietnam vets conducted by Patrick Boudewyns of the Augusta,
Georgia, Veterans' Administration Medical Center and the
Medical College of Georgia. In that study, EMDR® was found
to be more effective than standard group therapy. In fact, the
group therapy vets seemed to get a little worse.

These findings represent a breakthrough in the treatment
of PTSD, which was considered almost impossible to treat effectively, especially among Vietnam vets. The effects of the
war were so severe that *the suicide rate among combat vets was
higher than the number of war dead.* Therapists felt frustrated
with their limited ability to help these men and women who
had been reliving nightmarish scenes from the war for more
than two decades. They used a variety of behavioral techniques that required the vets to repeatedly imagine old,
painful scenes, which gave them only limited relief from
symptoms. With EMDR®, some vets are able to resolve their
difficulty with a particular memory in just one session.

Police officers, emergency service personnel, and others
who have suffered from the effects of trauma in the line of
duty have also gotten great relief from EMDR®. A study with
sixty such volunteers was conducted by Roger Soloman, Ph.D,
an internationally recognized expert in the recovery from witnessing or being the victim of such traumatic incidents as rob-
beries, shootings, or accidents. The participants attended a
stress debriefing to activate the memories of the incidents
and were then divided into two groups. The treatment group

received a brief EMDR® session focusing exclusively on the incidents. The other group received no treatment. On two-month and eight-month follow-ups, anxiety and distress in the EMDR® group was significantly lower than in the non-EMDR® group.

EMDR® has also helped disaster victims. In 1992, Hurricane Andrew crashed into the coast of South Florida and wreaked havoc on the physical and emotional lives of its residents. A team of EMDR® therapists volunteered their services to one hundred disaster survivors. Researchers who followed up with the victims three months after their treatment found that they continued to be free of PTSD symptoms. Because of the broad scope of its success, EMDR® has become recognized as a revolutionary therapy that is changing the field of psychotherapy.

THE BEST CANDIDATES FOR EMDR®

EMDR® therapists have successfully treated conditions stemming from a wide range of traumas such as rape, childhood physical and sexual abuse, loss of loved ones, and accidents, as well as chronic problems such as eating disorders, anxiety, low self-esteem from learning disabilities, blocked personal and professional performance, and dissociative disorders like multiple-personality disorder. EMDR® has also benefited general psychotherapy clients living dysfunctionally due to events from the past. And EMDR® therapists are getting excellent results with children.

While EMDR® has positive results with all of the above conditions, it works most rapidly with people dealing with symptoms from a single-incident trauma. This is *not* to say that EMDR® therapy is simply a "quick fix," for what appears to be a single-incident trauma might relate to a past event(s) which must also be cleared for symptom relief. In its broadest definition, a trauma is an experience that causes us to develop erroneous beliefs about ourselves or the world. For example, a child who is molested may come to believe she is bad and the world isn't safe. Traumatic experiences often become fixed both in the body and in the mind because they function together as an interconnected system. These effects on the body-mind can include irrational emotions such as low self-esteem or depression, blocked energy in the form of decreased motivation or general sluggishness, and physical symptoms ranging from digestive troubles to pain similar to that experienced during the incident.

Shapiro divides traumas into two types: minor traumas, which she calls "small t" traumas, and major or "big T" traumas. The "t" traumas are those experiences that lower our sense of self-confidence and assault our sense of self-efficacy. Like a perceptual filter, they narrow and limit our views of ourselves and the world and prevent us from living to our full potential. They also cause suffering. A client who came to me because she was having difficulties with her career and social life exemplifies "t" trauma. She had very low self-esteem, which she traced to her childhood as a fat little girl whose older brother and sister had teased relentlessly. A deep irrational belief that she was not good enough became embedded in her psyche. Even though she claimed, "I know I am smarter than most people," she always felt inferior to others. No matter how hard she tried, she just couldn't shake this feeling that controlled her self-concept and her approach to life.

The "T" traumas, such as rape, childhood physical and sexual abuse, natural disasters, accidents, and losses, affect us most dramatically. By damaging and jolting us, these traumas often engender debilitating symptoms of PTSD, including nightmares, flashbacks, anxieties, phobias, fears, and difficulties at home and work. Like the "t" traumas, they also affect our sense of self-confidence and self-efficacy.

It Helps to Have the Right Attitude

EMDR® works optimally with clients who are motivated to change. They must be ready to detach themselves from the past and experience life without their problems. But sometimes people are afraid to change. Perhaps they receive "secondary gains" from their problems and feel conflicted about letting them go. Some people depend on the benefits that come with their problems. Imagine the vet who has been disabled for years and counts on his monthly disability check, the accident victim who is suing for emotional distress, or the widow who thrives on pity. Although an initial impediment to the therapy, this kind of negative self-image can be effectively challenged by EMDR®.

EMDR® also works best for clients who are willing to allow themselves to feel uncomfortable feelings and think disturbing thoughts. As the EMDR® processing begins, clients' troubling memories are often intensified by the eye movements. The therapist instructs the client to stay with the feelings and refrain from doing anything to change them or make them go away. Occasionally the physical or emotional intensity becomes too much to tolerate, or people go "blank" and are unable to concentrate on the image. The EMDR® therapist can work through these sticking points and gradually enable the client to make progress.

EMDR® HAS ITS LIMITS

Although EMDR® has been successful for a broad spectrum of individuals with a wide variety of conditions, it does have limitations. Serious long-term problems like schizophrenia, deep-rooted personality disturbances, and obsessive-compulsive disorder have not responded as well to EMDR® therapy although we are learning how to work better with such problems and developing new protocols. These conditions take much longer to clear because they often have biological origins that may be combined with deep layers of multiple traumas. Although the results are not necessarily as dramatic as with single-incident trauma, EMDR® therapists are noting positive results with nearly everyone. People with cardiac or respiratory conditions also may not be suitable candidates for EMDR® therapy because of limitations on the amount of stress they can tolerate.

Occasionally, for a neurological reason, a person cannot process a memory. In other cases, a client is simply not willing to connect with his or her emotions; although the person may state a wish to do so, a psychological block prevents it. Client readiness is an important factor, for the person must be willing to venture deeply into unknown territory.

Sometimes a person's malaise cannot be traced to a specific target; consequently, the clinician cannot address a specific memory network for clearing. Chronic traumatic experiences are also difficult to treat. People whose problems stem from the deep conditioning of punitive parents or fundamentalist religious orders have difficulty letting down their defenses enough for EMDR®. One chronically depressed client, Daniel, felt cut off from life and from himself. He had been raised in a strict fundamentalist Christian family in which feelings were never expressed. Because of his upbringing, he developed a severe inner critic that perpetually judged him. Never allowing himself to let loose and enjoy life, he felt alienated and unhappy. During the EMDR® sessions, his critical part blocked out his feelings. He experienced brief shifts, but they didn't last. I believe that his early conditioning was too pervasive for EMDR® to be effective. After several months of slow progress, we reached a plateau. Because of his tendency to intellectualize rather than feel, I referred him to a therapist who specialized in working with the body as a means of accessing emotions.

Another client proved to be untreatable because he was determined never to lose control. Whenever I did the eye movements with him, he would say he felt fine, but I knew he was suppressing his experiences. His core belief that feelings should be repressed inhibited his motivation to change.

Some severely depressed clients get only partial relief from EMDR® because the cause of their depression is biochemical. Although EMDR® eases the impact of their traumatic memories, it does little to improve their mood. In this situation the EMDR® therapist should refer the client to a psychiatrist who can prescribe an antidepressant drug such as Prozac. Because these drugs have not been found to interfere with the EMDR® process, the client can continue the EMDR® therapy if appropriate.

Although these few examples illustrate the known limitations of EMDR®, they represent only a small percentage of individuals as compared to those who benefit enormously from the therapy.

The therapist's skill and experience with EMDR® can be a limitation to consider as well. How much experience has a therapist had with a certain type of problem? How long has the therapist been using EMDR®? Has the therapist used it with the specific problem a client is bringing? It is important to remember that EMDR® therapy is *not* the treatment of choice in every instance.

HOW DOES EMDR® PROCESSING WORK?

Several theories have been developed to explain what makes EMDR® processing work, but they have yet to be proven. In pursuit of the answers, researchers continue their studies and therapists gain knowledge by recording what they observe in their clients and in themselves when they are clients.

As I stated earlier, EMDR® is *not* simply "eye movements." Because EMDR® is a complex treatment that requires history-taking, client assessment, establishing a sound therapeutic relationship, and actual preparation for EMDR®, the EMDR® clinician must be thoroughly trained. Patterned eye movements are integrated with traditional talk therapy to remove or clear emotional, cognitive, and physical blockages. The premise is that clients' traumas have left a residue of unprocessed memories, feelings, and thoughts and that these can be targeted and processed or "metabolized" with specific eye movements. Similar to the way rapid eye movement

(REM) or dream sleep works, these eye movements help to process this blocked information, allowing the body-mind to release it.

Our dreams each night cleanse the body-mind of the day's residues. It seems that some particularly strong dreams related to past events are the body-mind's attempt to heal. However, during disturbing dreams the eye movements are often disrupted, and we awaken before REM sleep can complete its job. With EMDR® processing, though, the therapist keeps the client's eyes moving back and forth and guides the client into focusing on the traumatic event. This allows the event to be fully experienced and processed.

Some clients prefer to work with their eyes closed because they can focus inwardly more easily that way. A client may be blind or have eye problems. Some occasions mandate other means than eye movements to facilitate processing. For example, sometimes a client is crying too hard to watch the therapist's finger. In such situations, alternatively tapping a client's hands or knees or using sound bilaterally—for example, snapping one's fingers on either side of the client's head— are effective in stimulating the processing of material. These other forms of bilateral stimulation seem to create the same effect as the eye movements; and, in some cases, may be preferable. Although in this book I've stressed the use of eye movements, I often use other bilateral means of stimulation as well.

It may be that such stimulation dislodges the dysfunctional material that is lodged in the body-mind due to a small or large trauma. There is also a theory that the eye movements are associated with part of the brain called the hippocampus, which is linked to the consolidation of memory. Another theory is that the dual attention the client maintains with EMDR®, focusing simultaneously on the inner feelings and the eye movements, allows the alerted brain to metabolize whatever it is witnessing.

Eye movements have been used for hundreds of years by yoga practitioners to calm the mind. It may be that Shapiro not only rediscovered a basic biological mechanism for clearing the mind of present-time disturbances, but also ingeniously made the leap to linking the eye movements with stored psychological material. But, these are all just theories and it may take years to substantiate them with research.

ACCELERATED INFORMATION PROCESSING

The theory of accelerated information processing was developed by Shapiro to explain the rapid treatment effects that she observed with clients and to delineate the principles that guide the use of EMDR®. It seems that when a person experiences a trauma, either a "t" or "T," it becomes locked into its own memory network exactly as it was experienced—the images, physical sensations, tastes, smells, sounds, and beliefs—as if frozen in time in the body and the mind. A man who survives a train crash continues to have a fear of trains. The sight—and even the sound—of them makes him panic because all of the memories related to the accident are stuck in his nervous system. He has been unable to process them. Internal or external reminders of the crash will cause the experience to flash into his consciousness in its original form.

Ordinary events that we experience every day seem to pass through us without leaving much of a mark. Traumatic events, however, seem to get trapped and form a blockage. Like a broken record, they repeat themselves in our body-mind over and over again. Nightmares may actually be the mind's attempts to metabolize this trapped information, but the trauma memory always lasts beyond the dream. Perhaps this mechanism that freezes traumatic events was an adaptive device, helping to protect early humans from repeating mistakes. It could have served to keep our early ancestors alert so they would not be eaten by saber-toothed tigers. But, through our evolution this mechanism has become maladaptive: rather than protect us, it obscures our perceptions and emotions. For example, a young girl who is sexually abused by a man may fear all men, even as an adult. This fear can impede her ability to form a close relationship with a mate in adulthood, prevent her from having male friendships, and cause problems for her with male bosses in the workplace. Her anxiety around men may be very high and she may have no idea why.

In theory, the brain has an information-processing system which works toward keeping us in a balanced state of mental health, just as the body has a natural healing response to physical injury. Our bodies automatically go into action to heal a wound, but if something gets stuck in the wound, it will fester and resist healing. When confronted with a trauma, the nervous system gets stuck—as when a wound can't heal because it's dirty—and causes an ongoing array of PTSD symptoms.

To begin the EMDR® processing work, as part of the history taking, the therapist helps the client identify appropriate targets. This can take weeks, depending on both the clinician's skill and the client's readiness. To begin unblocking the system, the EMDR® therapist asks the client to focus on a "target" related to the trauma. The target could be a memory or dream image; a person; an actual, fantasized, or projected event; or a part of the experience such as a body sensation or thought. Accessing this target is an attempt to stimulate the memory network where the trauma is stored. Simultaneously, the eye movements or other stimuli appear to trigger a mechanism that restores the system's information processing abilities, enabling it to draw on information from a different memory network where the client will find insight and understanding. These two networks communicate information in a type of rapid free association called "accelerated information processing." Each set of eye movements further unlocks the disturbing information and accelerates it along an adaptive path until the negative thoughts, feelings, pictures, and emotions have dissipated and are spontaneously replaced by an overall positive attitude.

EMDR® works most rapidly with single-incident traumas because the client can easily identify a target. The target is analogous to a single log that is blocking the flow of a stream, causing a lot of damage. Removing that one log allows the river to flow naturally again. Likewise, clearing the targeted blockage allows the body-mind to return to its natural functioning. This is why EMDR® often gets dramatic results in one session. If the trauma is tied to other traumas, however, then they too must be cleared for the system to flow.

EMDR® VERSUS HYPNOSIS

Many people wonder about the difference between EMDR® and hypnosis. With hypnosis, a client who is reexperiencing a traumatic memory seems to process the entire event in real time, moment to moment, even when time distortion techniques are used. With EMDR®, the processing seems to go four to five times more rapidly. EMDR® is a state of accelerated processing wherein information from all parts of the system is accessed simultaneously. A client may only need to focus on a single scene of the trauma to fully process the entire event. For example, a mugging victim may focus only on the scene when he or she first became aware of the attacker and not need to replay the event scene by scene.

There is also much more client control with EMDR® than with hypnosis. Clients get spontaneous insights and new, healthy images without suggestions from the therapist. In fact, the therapist stays out of the client's way as much as possible, just following the process and allowing the natural healing to unfold.

The EMDR® Therapist

As with any treatment that can change people's lives, EMDR® in the hands of a therapist who is poorly trained or lacking in skills can cause damage. EMDR® can be likened to a power tool that when wielded by an inadequately trained person can do a lot of harm. EMDR® often opens clients in unexpected ways, which then requires a therapist's advanced skills for guidance. If necessary, a therapist may need to immediately end the session. It is imperative that the therapist be skilled and capable of assessing such a moment and in caring for the client. How to determine client readiness, to conduct EMDR® interviews correctly, timing, and the use of interweaves are taught in the advanced level of training. The latter method, which I discuss later in this chapter, requires great skill.

The use of EMDR® may exceed the ability of a new therapist with few skills and little experience. To have the minimal qualifications for using this therapy, therapists must have completed the full EMDR® training course. Shapiro has been criticized by some people in the field for restricting how this method is taught, but it would be irresponsible not to restrict untrained people from using this method. EMDR® is a very potent method which, if used by well-trained, competent clinicians, can be highly beneficial. If used by improperly trained people, however, it can create disastrous results. Because EMDR® breaks through defensive barriers, clients are often overwhelmed with traumatic images and emotions. Therapists must know how to work with this highly charged material. I have seen clients get trapped in hellish spaces, full of terror, and lose touch with reality. One client became so upset and caught up in reliving her traumatic memories that she mistook me for her perpetrator, jumped out of her chair, and cowered in the corner of my office. It took all of my clinical and intuitive abilities to get her back on track, reconnect with me, and continue to process the memory to the end.

There have been numerous accounts of people harmed by therapists who, without being trained in EMDR®, used eye movements on clients. Such accounts include stories of therapists who have opened clients to deeply disturbing material and then left the clients suspended in heavy emotion at the end of the session. Some such clients have become suicidal. Therapists who allow this to happen are behaving irresponsibly and unethically.

Taking the training alone does not guarantee that a ther-

apist will have all the skills necessary to practice EMDR®.
Many of my fellow facilitators and I have worked with therapists who have completed the training but still have not mas-
tered the protocol. Currently, there is no certification although
a proficiency assessment procedure is being developed by the
EMDR® Institute. (See Appendix A, How to Choose an
EMDR® Therapist.)

Along with good clinical skills and basic training in
EMDR®, a therapist should have a compassionate heart and
an ability to make a deep connection with clients. A caring
therapeutic relationship creates a space wherein clients can
feel safe opening up to deep, painful feelings and experiences.
This relationship is like a safety net or lifeline that allows
clients, knowing they will come out unscathed, to go to the
depths of shattering experiences from the past. They need to
know their therapist is attuned and responsive to their needs
and will guide them through the turbulence of processing
traumatic events. Although EMDR® may seem very techni-
cal, it is a highly intuitive process that should be tailored to
each client. Therapists must remain close enough to the
client's experience that they intuitively know what the client
needs.

Therapists must also be open-minded enough to objectively
look at their own beliefs about what can be healed by therapy
and how long it should take. Specifically, if a therapist believes
at least one year must pass before a person can healthily
emerge from grieving the death of a loved one, this limited
belief can seriously hinder the client's chances for full recovery in less time. Can the therapist accept that an abuse victim
can clear traumatic memories with EMDR® in only three
months? That a mother who has lost her child can recover in

two months? That an alcoholic has no need for AA because she quickly clears the traumas that caused her to use alcohol as a way of coping?

Therapists must also be willing to challenge their beliefs about when a process has been completed. For instance, a client might relax and sigh after several minutes of intense EMDR® processing work, but the client's shift does not necessarily mean that the client has completed his or her clearing work. I remember facilitating a training session for two therapists in which the "client" spent approximately thirty minutes processing a wide range of feelings associated with the death of his father. After the client emerged from intense sadness, the client and his "therapist" thought he was finished. The twosome would have stopped their work at that point, but I knew it might prove fruitful for him to explore further, thus challenging his belief that sadness was the end point. I encouraged him to continue the eye movements to see how far they could take him! After ten more minutes, he had moved through the sadness and felt love, joy, and peace.

EMDR® is a continually evolving method; it is being imaginatively integrated with almost every kind of therapy, from Gestalt to psychoanalytic psychotherapy. Even though all EMDR®-trained therapists learn the same basic protocols and procedures, they adapt their practice of the method to meet their own style and the individual needs of their clients.

ANATOMY OF AN EMDR® PROCESSING SESSION

A typical EMDR® treatment begins with a client's desire to heal from a trauma, eliminate a performance problem, or deal with a troubling aspect of life. The therapist's first step is to take a thorough history and get to know the person. Although this process usually takes a few sessions, sometimes it can be much longer. It is essential that a feeling of connection, caring, and safety be established between therapist and client. At that point, the EMDR® can begin.

Ninety minutes is the usual length of time for a session. Depending on the problem being treated, some clients do EMDR® processing in nearly every session, while others do it only occasionally. For a client working on traumatic child abuse, one ninety-minute EMDR® session may be followed by fifty minutes of talk therapy later that week to integrate the material that came up in the first session. Intensive EMDR® sessions in close succession can be the best method for other clients. One client came to me from another state to work on becoming free of his addiction to a self-destructive relationship. After four ninety-minute EMDR® sessions in one week, we had cleared his obsession. He returned home and got out of the relationship. A year later he told me the addictive pattern had never returned.

During EMDR®, the therapist acts as a facilitator or guide in the client's unfolding process. The following is a step-by-step description of that process, illustrated by excerpts of a dialogue from an actual EMDR® processing session I conducted with a woman named Renee.

Renee had felt depressed as long as she could remember and was experiencing problems in her intimate relationship. After reviewing her history I decided to begin the EMDR® processing with a traumatic memory that plagued her thoughts continuously and haunted her with nightmares.

Three years earlier she was canoeing on a river with some

friends. They were having a great time paddling leisurely down the river and occasionally jumping in the water for a refreshing swim. After they all smoked some marijuana and got very high, Renee swam out to a deep part of the river by herself, leaving her friends and the canoe by the river bank. She came upon a man splashing in the water. The next moment he went under. When he came up, she realized in her stoned stupor that he was drowning. Terrified, she called out to her boyfriend for help. The man went under a second time. Her boyfriend seemed to take his time removing his shoes and swimming to the drowning man, who was four feet in front of her. Everything was happening in slow motion. Before he went down for the third and last time, he looked at her straight in the eyes and cried, "help!" Paralyzed, she just stared at the empty place in the water. When the paramedics found his body far down the river, CPR was too late. Renee believed then and continued to believe that she had killed him. She was a murderer.

As Renee told me this story, she shuddered and turned pale. From that day she had been plagued by the image of the drowning man's face as he pleaded for help. Completely convinced of her guilt, she lived with the burden of this tragedy. Since the incident she would not go swimming and was especially afraid of cold water. Just being near water gave her a terrible feeling in the pit of her stomach and made her very shaky.

At the beginning of the first EMDR® session, I ask clients to identify and focus on a target related to the trauma. Then I ask for a life-limiting belief or "negative cognition" associated with the incident that has carried over to the present and affects their everyday life. Next, I ask for a "positive cognition"—a statement of what they would like to believe about themselves when they bring up the image. Then I have them tell me what emotions and physical sensations arise when they visualize that picture. My goal in this questioning is to stimulate the memory network in which the memory is locked so its various components can be processed. My session with Renee began as follows:

L: What image from the incident disturbs you the most?
R: The image of the man looking at me and saying "help!"
L: What do you believe about yourself when you look at that picture?
R: I killed him. (negative cognition)
L: What would you like to believe about yourself?
R: I did the best that I could. (positive cognition)
L: What do you feel in your body?
R: I feel spacey and frozen.

I then ask clients to rate how disturbing the target is on a scale from zero to ten. The "subjective units of disturbance" (SUDs) scale helps me to assess how much of the client's traumatic material has been processed. I take SUDs readings at different times during the processing to measure progress. After taking the initial SUDs rating, I ask the clients to bring up the disturbing image together with all of its related sounds and sensations and the negative cognition, to follow my fingers with their eyes, and to let whatever comes up arise without censoring it. Clients may experience images, body sensations, a range of emotions, insights, ordinary thoughts, or nothing much at all.

L: When you bring up the image of the man drowning and the thought "I killed him," how disturbing is it on a scale from zero to ten?

R: It's a ten.

L: Bring up the image of the man drowning, the thought "I killed him," and the sensations in your body, and follow my fingers with your eyes. Just let whatever happens happen. There are no right or wrong answers. We'll go for awhile and then I'll ask you to stop and to tell me what is happening. You can also stop at any time before I ask you to.

During the eye movements, clients go through a multidimensional free association of thoughts, feelings, and body sensations. Some go through an enormous range of experiences, including intense sensations; horrific images; strong emotions such as homicidal rage, overwhelming terror, grief, love, and forgiveness; possible memories, including descriptions attributed to prenatal and infancy experiences; and dream-like imagery rich in detail and symbolism. Throughout all of these experiences I tell clients to "stay with that" or "let it all just pass through" and reassure them that "this is old stuff." The EMDR® creates a very direct and thorough reexperiencing of the past as it was locked into the body-mind. Clients experience a "witness awareness," which enables them to allow the material to unfold with minimal interference.

Intuitively, I tune in to my clients and stay close to their experience. My fingers direct their eyes back and forth until I get an indication that they have finished processing a piece of information. The shift may be nearly imperceptible, but a therapist who is well-trained in EMDR® work will note it. If clients are very emotional, I keep their eyes moving until they become calm, allowing them to fully clear a part of the traumatic event. I also tell them to signal me at any time if they want to stop. Each client prefers a different speed and number of eye movements. Some do best with only ten or fifteen eye movements at a time; others like to go on for hundreds. After each round of eye movements I ask, "What is happening now?" or "What do you get now?" They report their experience and we move on to a new focus and more eye movements.

After a couple of minutes of eye movements, I checked in with Renee.

L: What's happening now?
R: I feel uncomfortable.
L: Go with that.

She continued her eye movements for six minutes.

L: What do you get now?
R: I feel water in my lungs, like it was me.

During another long set of eye movements, I could tell by her facial expressions that she was very involved in the processing.

L: What's happening now?
R: I don't know. . . . It's scary. I'm helpless. I want to do something but I can't. I'm not comfortable in the water. I'm swallowing water. I'm scared.

A memory arose that was related to the incident. When she was a little girl she and some friends used to go to a lake. They loved to jump off of the pier into the shallow water. One summer the water was much deeper than it had been previously, but they did not know it. A little girl about nine years old jumped in and the water went over her head. Unable to swim, she called out for help to the children watching from above. Renee jumped in to save her and found herself being drowned by the panicked girl. Using all of her strength, Renee managed to get the girl to the shore a short distance away. Both girls were exhausted and had swallowed a great deal of water. That day Renee learned the strength and danger of a drowning person.

L: How are you feeling now?

R: Scared.

L: Go with that. . . . What's coming up for you now?

R: A feeling of being stuck. I can't get out of it. The water is cold but not cold at the same time. (Her voice is slow and low. She is having a body memory of being stoned.) I'm stuck.

L: Go with the feeling of being stuck.

R: I feel a sense of weight. . . . If there wasn't this weight . . . I feel heavy and tense . . . I could do something. (She is experiencing more body memories, fully remembering the incident, her thoughts, and her sensations.)

L: Feel it now, the weight and tension.

R: I feel very tense.

This process of eye movements and check-in continues until the end of the session, when I go back to the image the client started with and remeasure the SUDs. When clients feel free of the emotional charge, reporting a SUDS of zero, I ask what they believe to be true now. This eliciting of a positive cognition at the end of the process is an important step in the EMDR® method. When the level of disturbance has been reduced all the way and the client is free from distress, I give her the opportunity to verbally express her new way of understanding and viewing herself. These positive cognitions must come only from the client and fit her subjective experience. They can include statements such as "I am safe now," "I did the best I could with what I knew at the time," and "It is in the past." I then "install" the positive cognition by asking the clients to think of that statement together with the previously distressing image (which often changes by becoming smaller or dimmer, black-and-white rather than color, or less threatening in some manner) and do a few sets of eye movements. This causes them to experience a totally new orientation to the image. At this point I always check to see if any new material emerges that needs to be processed. If there is, I either try to clear it in the same session or make a note of it and return to it next time.

L: Let's go back to the original picture, the image of the man looking at you and crying "help!" What do you get now? (I'm checking to see where she is in the processing. Has the picture changed?)

R: I see his face. I feel upset when I see his face.

L: Go with that.

R: I see his face and his eyes. I feel heavy.

L: What do you believe about yourself when you look at the picture now? (I'm checking to see if her beliefs about herself and the scene have changed.)

R: There was a man drowning and I was there. Physically there was nothing I could do. Basically there was nothing I could do. I feel stuck. (Her voice is sad and quite low, without a lot of expression.)

L: Go with "there was nothing I could do." (I knew that this was the truth about the situation. She personally could not save this man. She was not strong enough and she knew from the experience as a little girl that a drowning person is dangerous. Part of her knew that she could not save him, but the feeling of helplessness was overwhelming. By asking her to go with "there was nothing I could do," I was helping her to integrate what she knew to be true but had not fully accepted.)

R: There was nothing I could do. (Stated as a fact.) I feel some relief. Amazing! (She laughs as she fully appreciates what she now knows to be true.)

L: What do you believe about yourself now?

R: It was a terrible thing to watch. . . . It wasn't my fault and there was nothing I could do.

L: Go with that. (The positive cognition, "there was nothing I could do," is replacing the original negative cognition, "I killed him." She realizes in a very deep way that she did not kill him.)

R: It's like I'm a third person watching the scene. I see what is going on. . . . There is no blame or reproach. I feel detached. It doesn't feel as personal. (Her voice is calm and she is speaking matter of factly about what she is observing.) The whole thing was unfortunate. I don't feel guilty anymore. It's over. It was unfortunate. This is amazing!

L: When you bring up the picture now, how would you rate your feelings on a scale of zero to ten? (I am checking the SUDs level to see if she has cleared the trauma.)

R: I feel fine. A zero.

L: What's happening now?

R: I feel great! It still feels like I am viewing it from outside. It's over. There *was* nothing I could do.

Renee and I spent the last few minutes of the session talking about what she had experienced. She said she had approached EMDR® skeptically but was desperate to find anything that would relieve her suffering. She was completely surprised that the therapy had worked. I advised her to keep track of her dreams, thoughts, and feelings during the following week. We would address anything of importance in the next session.

When she came in the next week, Renee cheerfully reported that she had gone river rafting over the weekend and "had a blast." This was the first time she had been on a river since the traumatic incident, and she had no trace of the old feelings. She said she felt happy, relieved, and appreciative. Several months later she let me know she was still feeling terrific.

Although Renee underwent a complete turnaround after just one EMDR® session, this is often not the case with other clients. If a client has not cleared his or her problem by the end of the first session, I use a variety of methods to "close it down." By closing down, I ensure that the client is fully reoriented to the present moment and feels solidly in his or her physical body; it is essential that a client feels self-contained and that he or she will not fall apart emotionally after leaving my office. Creating a sense of closure is crucial for the client's well-being because EMDR® brings up highly-charged material that can leave him or her very vulnerable. If the client is not properly closed down, he or she can become overwhelmed with emotion, suicidally depressed, unable to function at home or work, and afraid to continue the EMDR® or any other kind of therapy. I tell some clients it's a good idea to walk around the block before driving and perhaps not return to work for the day.

The processing of material often continues on its own between EMDR® sessions. I advise all of my clients to facilitate this natural processing by recording their dreams and insights in a journal, as well as drawing, painting, or engaging in other kinds of artwork. To help them cope better with stress that may arise, I often teach meditation and stress reduction techniques.

INTERWEAVES: AIDS TO JUMP-START INFORMATION PROCESSING

There are times when using the eye movements and following the client's process are not sufficient to keep the information flowing to a positive resolution. Clients sometimes enter into cognitive or emotional loops, repeating the same thoughts or feelings (or both) over and over. At these times the therapist must use "interweaves," a proactive EMDR® strategy that serves to jump-start blocked processing, to introduce information rather than depend solely on what arises from the client. The statements or images the therapist offers serve to weave together memory networks and associations that the client was not able to connect. Interweaves introduce a new perspective and new information or information that the client "knows" but does not have access to in the state of mind that is activated. There are many interweave methods and the selection of the appropriate method is mandated by the specific situation. Traumatic experiences often seem to be stored in one part of the body-mind without being affected by more current information. The interweaves create a bridge between the parts of the client's mind that have been separated. After the interweave is introduced the processing begins to flow again.

Interweaves are particularly effective with adults traumatized as children, who seem to relate to the experience completely from the child's perspective. This was the case with Louisa. Louisa was brutally physically and sexually abused by her older teenaged brothers when she was a young girl. We had reached an impasse in her processing because she believed that she was bad. In fact, she was so convinced of her "badness" that she was ashamed to proceed. Her child self fully believed that Louisa was bad because of what had been done to her. The rule in Louisa's family was, "If something bad happened to you, it was your fault because you allowed it to happen."

Because I knew that Louisa dearly loved her nine-year-old niece, I asked Louisa to suppose that her niece was being treated in the same way Louisa had been. If that were the case, would Louisa believe her niece was bad? Louisa emphatically exclaimed, "No!"

Now I realized that she had engaged her adult self and with that I directed Louisa to resume the eye movements. Her two memory networks linked immediately and she blurted, "My brothers were the bad ones. I was just an innocent child."

Interweaves are also helpful with traumatic events that have become frozen in the body. During nearly every EMDR® session, clients feel both a mental and a physical shift. The physical shift can be experienced as a release of tension, a feeling of energy, or a sense of things leaving. Melanie had been suffering from chronic back pain since childhood and was searching for its origins. A nearly crippling lower back condition prevented her from walking more than a short distance and working in her cherished garden. At my urging she went to an orthopedist and began an exercise program. But, the exercises didn't help. During one of our sessions Melanie noticed that the back pain got worse during and after the EMDR®. Using the pain as our target, I asked her what she believed about herself. She said she believed there was something in her lower back. I told her to go with that belief, along with the sensation, as she moved her eyes back and forth. Melanie immediately regressed to her child state and said, echoing her adult belief, "There is something in my back." We continued the eye movements to process that feeling and out came the sensation and imagery of her uncle anally raping her as a child. Her child self believed that the perpetrator's penis was still in her rectum. We explored how the penis could be removed and came up with the idea that her trusted female gynecologist could do it. I told her to imagine that removal as she moved her eyes back and forth. (I was interweaving a healing image.) She reported with glee that the doctor had rid her of the ugly atrophied penis and thrown it in the trash. After I told her to think about that and move her eyes again, she said, "The penis is gone from my back and the pain is gone." She was ecstatic! A year later Melanie was still free of pain and was an active hiker and gardener.

These case histories show that EMDR® clears locked-in damaging information from both the body and the mind *without removing anything that is useful or necessary.* A molestation victim, for example, will no longer be plagued by nightmares and flashbacks of the traumatic events, but she will not forget that it happened. Instead of believing that no one can be trusted, she comes to know that *some* people can be trusted. According to Francine Shapiro, "When the information is positively integrated and adaptively resolved, it is available for future use. EMDR® doesn't take away anything that's supposed to be there and it doesn't give a person amnesia." A basic principal of EMDR® therapy is that basic health resides within all of us. EMDR® removes blockages caused by negative images, beliefs, and body sensations and allows this natural state to shine through.

CHAPTER 3

Beyond Recovery

Heart beating rapidly, a young woman is crying and tense. She is reprocessing a horrifying and humiliating memory of being held down on a bed at the age of six by two strange men. One forces her knees apart and penetrates her painfully. As she moves with sets of eye movements through this profoundly disturbing memory, she successively experiences fear, guilt, anger—and suddenly, she is calm. She sighs, then smiles. She reports she realizes that those men have been dead for a long time and she will never see them again. Following her next set of eye movements, she says she is going to be okay. She does another set of eye movements after which she matter-of-factly states that her body is just a shell that can be molded but that her soul is beautiful and untouched from this experience. By the end of the session she understands that she is more than her body; the original scene no longer disturbs her and she feels calm when she recalls it.

My EMDR® colleagues and I love to share our experiences of inspirational transformations we have witnessed in our offices. I have spoken with therapists from around the world about what I have witnessed in my office and have found them equally eager to share their moving stories of spiritual and psychological transformation. Each of us has been awed by the kinds of transformations our clients have experienced in our presence. However, we have been reticent to report these in the research literature or press because of our concern that EMDR® might be seen as "California New Age" and impair EMDR®'s legitimacy as a valuable therapeutic method.

I believe that what we are witnessing as part of the EMDR® experience fits with the theory that explains how EMDR® functions. As described in Chapter 2, theoretically, EMDR® returns us to a natural balance or wholeness. When we remove dirt from a wound, the body's natural forces mobilize to heal the injury; when EMDR® clears blockages to the body-mind's natural healing, wholeness and balance are restored, which are experienced as peace, equanimity, joy, understanding, wisdom, love, and compassion. EMDR® clears impediments to wholeness, yet never removes what is adaptive and functional. Anger, fear, grief, and aversion are cleared, and the outcome of an EMDR® session is always a feeling of calm, peace, or love. These feelings increase with further eye movements whereas anger, fear, etc. continue to dissipate.

EMDR® has expanded my view of what is possible. I believe that our essential nature is clarity, wisdom, and compassion and that our conditioning obscures our knowing of our essence. Consequently, we don't express our true essence. As we grow older, we define ourselves by beliefs and concepts and take these to be the true story about who we are. If our essential nature is like the sun, it is as if the sky becomes cloudy, causing the sun to disappear. In truth, our sun is never gone; it is simply hidden. EMDR® processing clears the clouds, revealing the sun.

In EMDR® processing, many clients actually *experience*

the clarity, compassion, and understanding that is their true nature. Often, words of wisdom tumble from a client's mouth and the client is astounded at hearing them. An upwelling of love for self and others is frequently experienced in EMDR® processing sessions.

Love, peace, wisdom, understanding, and wholeness are our birthright and natural state of being. This chapter outlines the full range of powerful and often unexpected effects of EMDR®, which are further detailed in the following chapters.

EMDR® AND PSYCHOLOGICAL MEMORY

EMDR® seems to work by clearing what Jean Klein refers to as "psychological memory," memory that feels emotionally charged, alive in the present, and very personal. Enormous energy and tension are employed thinking about and maintaining a psychological past, and these memories form the basis for our personal identity: we believe we are our history. Our bodies and minds hold these memories which imprison us. By identifying with them we cannot live fully in the present.

For example, Melissa, a forty-five-year-old woman, was profoundly affected and haunted by the image of her beloved mother dying in the hospital. Melissa was twelve years old at the time. The emotional pain of her loss gave rise to the belief that "it isn't safe to love someone because you can lose them," and Melissa founded much of her life on this premise. She had difficulty in interpersonal relationships and refused to allow intimacy in any relationship. Whenever she would start to get too close to a partner, Melissa found a reason to end the relationship or cause her partner to leave. Melissa's pain mounted and severely affected her self-esteem. Images of her failed relationships, along with beliefs such as "I am inadequate" or "I am incapable of having a healthy long-term relationship," formed new layers of her self-identity. Consequently, she developed a lifestyle and career that made having a long-term committed relationship difficult if not impossible. Her self-concept was quite limited.

EMDR® therapy goes to the origins of such limiting life patterns and clears them by working with the target memories and negative self-beliefs. Frequently, the outcome of a completed EMDR® session is an "objective memory." Objective memories no longer possess an emotional charge, and traumatic events from the past are remembered simply as facts. The memories are no longer alive in the present; rather, they are experienced as belonging to the past. After EMDR® sessions clients typically report that long-term disturbing memories (psychological memories) no longer seem to belong to them and say, "It is over" or "It is like reading about it in the newspaper." Old memories, including memories of terrible abuse, cease to feel personal to the client. Instead of feeling "It happened to me," a client will feel "It happened." The shift is from "These are my memories" to "These are memories." Clients can simply acknowledge that these things happened (objective memory) and release them rather than identify with their histories.

For instance, Jane, a twenty-nine-year-old nurse who had been molested by her father as a child, reported after three months of intensive EMDR® therapy—during which time she reprocessed memories of the abuse—that whenever the memory resurfaced, it was no longer a problem. For many people, the feeling of it being "my life" or "my memory" becomes simply, "it happened." Clients don't typically forget what happened to them—it just doesn't seem as important any more.

Melissa, whom I mentioned earlier, reported at the end of an EMDR® session that when she recalled the image that represented the loss of her mother, the image no longer felt painful—it felt in the distant past. Melissa felt compassion for her child self because she had suffered such a loss. Furthermore, Melissa realized the damage that image had wrought on her relationships with men and the structure of her life and she replaced that dysfunctional belief with one that felt totally true to her: The loss of her mother was in the past and Melissa could love and be loved.

Oftentimes, at the end of an EMDR® session clients view the image of the original traumatic event as if from above the scene; they see themselves as part of the scene but no longer as the center of it. They see that they are just a part of the whole picture. This view totally reorients them: Their personal point of view globalizes and causes previously held patterns of behavior and beliefs to release and shift.

An example of this shift to a global perspective was given in Chapter 1 when I recounted working with the image of my father being angry with me for wetting my pants. In that session I processed the terror I had felt and the belief that I was responsible for his anger. If you recall, at the end of the session, I was astonished at how my perspective shifted: I sensed that I was just a part of a much greater whole. I viewed my family history from above, not visually, but perceptually. No longer in the center of the experience, I was but a participant in something greater than any of the individuals involved.

OBJECTIVE FORGIVENESS

Commonly, "objective forgiveness" results from the complete reprocessing of a traumatic event and signifies that the psychological memory has shifted to objective memory. Objective forgiveness is not a sentimental kind of forgiveness but, rather, an unemotional comprehension of why someone harmed the client. Often, understanding and peace replace the desire for revenge or justice. At this point the person feels that the past is indeed in the past.

At the end of the EMDR® session I perceived that my father's actions stemmed from his own suffering as a result of rejection and mistreatment by his cold, unloving mother. At the session's end, I was no longer angry. Nor did I desire an apology. I felt that his anger at me was in the far distant past. Actually, my father seemed very different to me as an adult. He was no longer the threat to me I'd felt as a child, and he was happier. In a way, we had both suffered similar experiences of rejection from our parents.

In objective forgiveness, objectivity prevails. It is acceptance, not resignation, and this kind of forgiveness creates a kind of inner peace.

Objective forgiveness applies to oneself as well as to others. So often people suffer with lifelong regret and feelings of self-blame: the veteran who was able to save two comrades but not a third, the mother who did not stop her husband from abusing her children, the railroad worker who couldn't stop the train before it struck a car carrying a family of four, or the adult who as a child sexually abused his younger sister. Self-hate, guilt, and condemnation impede emotional healing;

with the full clearing of a traumatic event clients understand why they acted as they did, experience it as in the past, and then experience themselves more fully in the present.

For example, a police officer ridden with guilt because he was not able to push his partner out of the way of a gunman's lethal bullet realized that *he had done the best he could at the time*. This was not an intellectual rationalization but a statement that he experienced as totally true and releasing. Relief coursed through him as he stated this realization, and he felt at peace with himself for the first time in a long while. He then felt he could move on with the rest of his life.

In the case of perpetrators, or people who have knowingly harmed others, you may question whether self-forgiveness is such a good idea. What we have found with EMDR® therapy is that a person is able to take responsibility for past action and express a desire to make amends. Perpetrators recognize that they cannot change the past but can do positive things in the present.

CHANGES IN CORE BELIEFS AND UNDESIRABLE BEHAVIOR PATTERNS

As EMDR® therapy transforms psychological memory to objective memory, core negative beliefs about oneself and the world are also transformed. Abuse victims who have lived with beliefs that they are bad, dirty, unlovable, shameful, and can never trust anyone have experienced these beliefs to be invalid and based on past misperceptions. Beliefs such as "I'm okay," "I am lovable," "I am honorable," and "I can trust some people" spontaneously replace old negative constructs and effect a shift in self-perception and self-worth. Chronic sufferers from low self-esteem due to traumatic events during childhood have experienced major increases in positive self-esteem.

Similarly, many EMDR® clients experience marked behavioral shifts. Unhealthy behavior patterns desist and new appropriate behavioral responses emerge once EMDR® has cleared the emotional obstruction from the person's system. The following account of a thirty-two-year-old woman's experience illustrates how changes in beliefs and behavior are brought about spontaneously through the processing of an old memory.

In my first EMDR® experience I chose a persistent memory of me as a young child and my mother walking down some concrete stairs at the community pool. In the memory I have my towel wrapped around my body, including my arms. My mother is looking down at me telling me to leave my arms free and relating a story of some other little girl who had fallen down some stairs. This little girl could not catch herself because she was bound up by her towel and fell right onto her head.

As the most disturbing image of this memory, I chose an image of me tumbling helplessly down the stairs that day at the pool. While I had not *actually* fallen down the stairs, this image had remained with me ever since my mother told me that story—I felt on some level as if it had really happened to me.

The negative cognition attached to this image was "I am out of control of my life," my longstanding belief. Thus, at this point, nothing arose for me of which I was not already aware. Once I began the eye movements, however, I clearly entered into what Francine Shapiro calls accelerated process-ing. In a very short period I moved from cowering fear to rage that wanted to attack and then to an empowered centeredness that did *not* need to attack. Along with this rising sense of em-powerment, I felt a great deal of sexual energy and was star-tled by this connection.

As I continued processing this target memory, initially I felt confused and frustrated because the image of me as a little girl tumbling down the stairs did not shift. What began to happen, however, was my gaining an increasing sense of dis-tance from the image—as if I were receding from it. I said to my therapist that I was still disturbed that the little girl was falling but somehow I was not feeling frightened anymore. She [therapist] had me go with that experience and contin-ued with the eye movements. In the middle of this set, I was suddenly struck by the realization that *the little girl falling down the stairs was not me but my mother!* I began to laugh and felt a great wave of relief. The positive cognition "I am competent and in control of my life" settled almost immedi-ately in my center, and I really *felt* it. It felt totally true to me.

The realization that much of my sense of anxiety and lack of control was simply the result of my having internalized my *mother's experience* was most definitely a new one for me. Even more significant, however, was the distinction I experi-enced in the EMDR® process. I was separate from my mother. And, as the result of the separation, a greater sense of control and empowerment has stayed with me.

Not long after this particular EMDR® session I visited my parents' home for Christmas. *I noticed almost straightaway that I felt a new sense of boundary between myself and my mother. I saw her anxiety as her own and was not habitually trying to calm her down. I was able to contact my own center and rest there.*

Felt Sense of Truth

I have found that EMDR® helps clients get more in touch with a bodily sense of "rightness" or "truth." Clients develop an attunement to their own inner wisdom, which they had been taught to censor or discount as children. The EMDR® process supports and nurtures the development of this suppressed body-centered knowing.

In EMDR® therapy the therapist follows and facilitates the client's process. If the therapist gives a suggestion or an affirmation that doesn't feel true to the client, it is immediately rejected; the level of distress will not decrease until what is introduced fits. Only something that fits can enter the system. In this way clients learn to attune to their bodies and minds and to feel what is true for them.

An important step in the EMDR® method is the installation of a positive cognition, which helps to instill this body-based knowing. The positive cognition, as you may recall, is a positive statement about oneself (a "self statement") that is elicited from the client at the end of an EMDR® session when the level of disturbance has been reduced and the client is free from distress. The positive cognition is a new way of understanding or viewing oneself and when paired with the original distressing picture the client experiences a totally new orientation to that event.

The EMDR® method is based on following a client's reported experiences and simply and objectively honoring what is true for the client. This, in turn, enables clients to observe and report on their experiences with less judgment and aversion, listening to themselves and basing actions on that information rather than preconditioning. Clients often report feeling as if a puzzle piece were falling perfectly into place. In EMDR® therapy, clients develop and strengthen their sense of truth or inner wisdom.

Rosemary, a forty-five-year-old secretary, benefited notably in this respect. As a child, she had been sexually abused by a female relative. When Rosemary entered therapy, she was having nightmares about her family thinking she was "crazy" and sending her away to a mental hospital. These extremely upsetting dreams caused her a great deal of anxiety and distress during the day. After processing the dream in an EMDR® session, she revealed her concern about seeing the abuse perpetrator at an upcoming family gathering; Rosemary felt out of control and crazy in her anticipation of seeing this person. It appeared that much of Rosemary's distress occurred because no one in the family knew about the abuse and regarded the guilty family member as loving and kind. I suggested that she think of one person in the family she could tell about the abuse and then imagine telling that person. As Rosemary moved her eyes, her anxiety which had been cycling very high dropped completely to a feeling of calm. She felt a puzzle piece fit: She knew that by telling someone else, someone else would know Rosemary wasn't crazy.

I have found that many of my clients are increasingly able to integrate this felt sense of rightness into their daily lives. They develop an inner sense of whom they can trust and a feeling of correct judgment. They become more sensitive to a bodily sense of right or wrong and learn to trust and listen to their body wisdom.

Trust in Life and Self-confidence

I have found that many EMDR® clients develop greater trust in life and an increased ability to fully experience whatever life brings. The EMDR® method seems to enable clients to disidentify with their history objectively (that is, it is no longer felt as personal) and allows them to face difficult feelings and thoughts. As a result, EMDR® therapy can move rapidly and can model an approach to life. Clients can let an experience pass through their awareness and can "be with it" just as they were able to do in EMDR® sessions. Clients become more adept at rapidly recognizing behavior patterns and either process them on their own without EMDR® or bring them to sessions.

Many of my EMDR® clients come to understand what Alan Watts called "the wisdom of insecurity." They learn that they can be with whatever arises without having to control or defend against it. Just as they learned to trust the unfolding process in their EMDR® therapy—to go through the most intense difficult feelings and think the unthinkable thoughts—so are they more able to trust what arises in their lives. I have seen clients with terrible histories of abuse open to their lives in new ways, no longer needing to control their experience. They learn that they can "be" with whatever arises.

This deepening trust in the ability to deal with painful emotions is illustrated in the case of Barbara, a thirty-six-year-old woman who worked through the intense feelings of fear and helplessness she experienced between the ages of two and three while being molested by her teenage brother. Although

Barbara had undergone conventional therapy in the past, she had avoided working on her incest memories. She sought EMDR® therapy as a last ditch effort: her husband was threatening to leave her, in part because of her emotional aloofness.

Barbara had always feared and avoided her feelings. Using EMDR® processing she was able to enter and emerge from her worst fears and memories feeling better. For the first time since the abuse, she could fully feel her body. In addition, she realized she would be all right if her husband should leave her. She told me, "I know I'd be okay. I'm no longer as afraid of being alone. I can go through the feelings."

Her success in handling such intense emotions during our EMDR® sessions increased her confidence and instilled a body-based knowing that she could allow other emotions to pass through her body-mind too. Now that she had survived reexperiencing the incest trauma and felt "okay" afterward, she knew she could emerge successfully from feelings of grief and loss.

Such self-confidence and empowerment seem to be universally experienced by EMDR® clients, who also become much more autonomous than clients in more traditional therapies. EMDR® therapists rely a great deal on the client's inner experience and direct little attention to transference issues or what is happening in the client-therapist relationship. Consequently, clients feel less dependent on their therapists because clients feel their healing and insights have come from themselves rather than from an external source.

Therapists who use EMDR® must be willing to venture into unknown territory; they must be comfortable with not knowing what is going to happen next. Often when I work with clients, I do not have a specific anticipation of what is going to emerge from them. Yet, I know that if I can facilitate the continuation of the processing of experiences and guide the client out of stuck places, then I can rely on a wisdom inherent in the process. If I can keep the client's process moving, what needs to happen next can occur.

For example, Karen was experiencing terrible postpartum depression and having intrusive fantasies and thoughts about harming her baby. During an EMDR® session, her fear arose that she would stab her baby with a knife. She was very disturbed and wanted to block out this thought and imagery. Calmly, I instructed her to go with the image of stabbing her baby. As she imagined stabbing her baby, she sobbed deeply— and then, suddenly, began laughing. After the set she told me that as she stabbed her baby, the baby kept laughing and smiling at her as if nothing had happened. Karen realized, "I can't hurt my baby," and felt an enormous surge of relief. When I had instructed her to imagine stabbing her baby, I had no idea what would emerge; but past experience has taught me to trust that whatever arose for Karen needed to come up and be released for her healing.

Many of my EMDR® clients begin to approach life with an openness and freshness and rely less on their personal history when making decisions. They look at all facets of a situation—including what they experience in their bodies and minds—and find that the solution arises spontaneously. Consequently, clients develop greater trust in life, and their anxiety and worry about the future decreases.

I watched this evolution occur in Lisa, a young woman who had been sexually abused as a child. In our work together she noticed her depressed and hopeless feelings and made a great deal of progress in releasing the past. At different times I suggested to her that she might benefit from joining other women with similar histories in a group, but she had always refused, feeling she was not yet ready. Finally, although she was still somewhat anxious, she felt ready to participate in the group and she felt right about her timing.

Profound Energy Releases

Clearing old psychological material can profoundly affect energy in the body. In fact, clients commonly report feeling energy "shifting" in their bodies during and after sets of eye movements. Sometimes I see these energy shifts manifest as increased or decreased breathing, crying, laughing, shaking, or deep sighs—a noticeable relaxation response—and when a client has freed her- or himself from disturbing psychological memories, she or he often feels a lightness and spaciousness in body and mind. Many clients experience their bodies tension-free for the first time in their lives.

One client likened the feeling to cement blocks leaving her body. Others have told me that they feel energy coursing through their bodies, that something "blocked" in their head, heart, throat, or solar plexus has been unblocked, and that blissful energy is rising up their spines. Many energy shifts have been quite dramatic.

Amy, a pleasant fifty-five-year-old manager, was troubled by low self-esteem, low self-confidence, and a lack of sexual desire. In an EMDR® session with me, she identified a significant memory of her father molesting her when she was twelve years old. While processing that memory, Amy realized that she was pulling in her energy around her genital area; she believed, "My energy is dangerous, my energy is bad." She realized that as a child she believed *she* had caused her father to molest her and so made the decision to restrain her energy. In our session she could literally feel herself withholding her energy and realized that her erroneous belief had inhibited her creatively, intellectually, and sexually.

She focused her attention on her reproductive organs and genitals as she moved her eyes back and forth and soon reported feeling her energy shifting. "I can feel my ovaries," she commented. By the end of the session she reported that the energy had moved and "opened up" the area of her reproductive organs. Now she believed, "It was my father's responsibility to control himself. I can open to my energy." Amy was delighted and reported feeling much more empowered.

In our next session she told me she had continued to feel energy shifts. Furthermore, her acupuncturist—whom she had been seeing concurrently with our work—was very impressed and had been noticing major changes in her energy. EMDR® work had unblocked previously obstructed places in her system and had resulted in increased vitality, energy, and self-confidence.

Reports that energetic blockages, particularly in the heart area, have been released are commonplace at the completion of EMDR® sessions. Clients experience warmth and openness, which manifest in feelings of compassion for themselves and others. It appears that memories, dysfunctional behaviors, and beliefs create blockages in the body's naturally flowing energy system and EMDR® clears the blockages on all of these levels, thus restoring the body's natural energy flow. This natural flow of energy is experienced as peace, love, openness, and joy. This is our birthright. When the psychological blockages to the flow are removed, we come to our natural way of being.

TRANSFORMATIVE SPIRITUAL AND PARANORMAL EXPERIENCES

Typically, clients feel a deep calm and spaciousness following the complete processing of a disturbing life event. Some speak of spiritual insights, profound experiences of peace, love, and joy, or a connection with the miracle of life. Even spontaneous openings to the psychic realm have occurred for clients who had no previous interest or experience in it.

I have had many clients who, after completing most of the clearing of past disturbing material, begin to ask bigger life questions and take a strong interest in spirituality. They realize increasingly that *they* are not their memories that comprise the "I" concept. But who are they? "I know what I am not," reported one client who had processed an enormous amount of extremely disturbing memories, "but I don't know who I am." Another client had completely abandoned her traditional religious faith as a child because it felt empty and meaningless to her when her younger sister died. Since clearing most of her terrible memories, she has developed a deep sense of spirituality.

Karen, mentioned earlier, was a young, self-described workaholic with a new baby. She too connected with newfound spirituality after EMDR® work. Though Karen was afraid of dying, she had scary thoughts of killing herself. As she performed the eye movements, I instructed her to imagine killing herself. She did so and finally saw herself dead. At that moment, a profound sense of peace and calm filled her and immediately, for the first time, she desired to pursue her spirituality. Karen realized her compulsive work habits occupied her mind and thus protected her from facing the questions of her own mortality of which she was terrified. Thus, her compulsivity separated her from her deepest self. In her EMDR® session, Karen's fear of death abated and without that fear controlling her, Karen chose to slow down and enjoy her baby, to work fewer hours, and to develop a spiritual life. This understanding and insight came to her spontaneously.

As discussed earlier, EMDR® helps clients see that they are not their histories or stories. In many current therapeutic approaches, clients identify themselves as survivors of one sort or another—a very constricting identity because we are *not* our past. Identification with the past binds us to it, whereas letting go of the identification frees us.

I worked intensively over a three-month period with Betty, who was struggling with an early history of sexual abuse, physical abuse, and her mother's addiction to prescription painkillers. After processing most of these memories with EMDR®, Betty was still very upset by, in her words, "a very sad life story." When she said that, I instructed her to "think about it as a story," while she did another set of eye movements. In that set, her internal scene shifted. She saw a mother reading a sad story—Betty's life story—to a little girl. Despite the sadness, the two of them went on to do something else. At this point, Betty experienced a tremendous shift in her body and mind and felt a pervasive sense of deep understanding and release. She realized she had created a *story* about her life; her story was not life itself. Betty felt released from the self-imposed limitation when she disidentified with the story as her life. Yes, her story was sad, but it did not define her essence. She returned for one more session, our closing session, and during it, exuded a sense of peace, equanimity, and joy.

Some of my clients have had spontaneous openings to psychic or paranormal experiences during our EMDR® sessions. Clients have suddenly "seen" dead loved ones surrounded by light and communicated with them. Such experiences have assuaged grief and left the clients feeling deep peace of mind and heart. One client developed clairsentient powers, the intuitive ability to feel what others feel. She had never had any interest in psychic phenomenon and was quite surprised by this ability. She has since gone on to develop this intuitive gift more fully.

These experiences emerged spontaneously without any direction from me. Neither did I interpret them. Rather, I allowed the clients to find their own meaning. When asked by a surprised and shocked client what her experience meant, I asked, "What does it mean to you? How is this experience acting on you? Live with it and then tell me what you have noticed." I can't pretend to know what the meaning is for a given client. My responsibility is to stay out of my clients' way and allow them to discover what these experiences mean to them. For each client the experience had a profound, personal, and life-changing meaning.

CHAPTER 4

Rapid Recovery from Trauma

Traumatic events like accidents, rapes, violence, and disasters can have a devastating effect on a person's life. These events may cause us to change our views about ourselves and our world and shake the foundation upon which we have built our lives. After being mugged, for instance, a formerly self-confident and secure man may become fearful, dependent, and mistrustful. Previously outgoing and gregarious, he may be increasingly withdrawn and reclusive now and avoid anything that reminds him of the mugging. He may feel ashamed for not having done something to prevent the mugging and may experience a drop in his self-esteem. Furthermore, he may suffer recurrent nightmares and flashbacks.

Traumatic incidents affect more than the individuals directly involved. Friends and loved ones of the victims often suffer the ripple effects of the incident. In the above example, the man who was mugged may take his anger out on his wife. He may have difficulty being intimate with her because of his disturbing thoughts and feelings. He may not want to socialize with friends anymore because of his feelings of shame and fear. Difficulty in concentrating may impair his work, and he may lack motivation.

Prior to EMDR®, therapists found that although clients might experience some desensitization by talking about a traumatic event, disruptive thoughts, images, and behaviors resisted change. Many clients I have helped with EMDR® had worked unsuccessfully in more traditional therapy and, although they had achieved some desensitization, emotional reactivity remained.

There is a major belief embedded in our culture that once you have experienced a trauma, you are damaged for life and must live with the outcome—it can be like learning to cope with life without an arm or a leg. EMDR® work has completely changed my view about the extent and speed of healing. Certainly, after being the victim of a crime or a major disaster, one changes. We learn from everything that happens to us. However, what is different with EMDR® is that the *feeling of being permanently damaged disappears. The feeling and belief of being a victim of any kind vanishes.* The traumatic event loses its emotional charge, and erroneous beliefs and unhealthy behaviors cease.

Besides clearing the trauma from the entire system, EMDR® *works very quickly.* In many cases when the traumatic event was an isolated incident, I have found that the traumas were cleared in *one* EMDR® session. Furthermore, I have repeatedly witnessed many people, both in my office and at EMDR® trainings, resolve—in a very short time—lifelong problems that originated from a single trauma.

EMDR® is a "time-free" therapy in the sense that it doesn't matter how long ago the trauma occurred. Because our nervous system stores the trauma in the present time, a World War II veteran can receive relief from his nightmares just as a Vietnam or a Desert Storm veteran can. It does not matter when the trauma was initially experienced; all emotional charge dissolves in the same way.

What follows are three remarkable and inspiring stories of recovery from devastating traumas. Each woman experienced relief from her symptoms after only one EMDR® processing session. In each case I had been seeing the client either as part of an ongoing course of therapy prior to using EMDR® on the incident or continued to see the client for a short time for other issues.

Veronica's Story

Veronica was a bright, perky, talkative nineteen-year-old woman who came to see me at the urging of her concerned mother. Although Veronica had seen another therapist for a short time for her problem before coming to me, Veronica reported that her problems had not diminished.

On Veronica's first visit to me she plunked down on my couch, crossed her long legs, and immediately began to relate the story of what brought her to see me. She was eager to get the help she so desperately needed, and a comfortable rapport immediately developed between us.

The youngest of five children—all girls, Veronica grew up in a comfortable middle-class neighborhood. Both of her parents were professionals who worked outside the home. Although she appeared self-assured, her easygoing demeanor belied the fear and anxiety she lived with on a daily basis. She was afraid to be alone anywhere and had had problems sleeping at night for as long as she could remember. She would awaken with a rush of adrenaline at the slightest sound. Some nights she awoke frequently because their old house creaked, and sounds made by nocturnal animals or the wind made it difficult for her to get back to sleep.

Veronica repeated an elaborate checking ritual before going to bed. Carrying a heavy baseball bat, she would check every nook and cranny in the house. She'd lock all of the windows, bolt the doors, and close all of the blinds. She would even check in the shower. Despite her checking, an uneasy feeling that someone was watching her hung over her, and she didn't feel safe. She slept with the light on in her room. "Nothing can make me feel safe," she despaired.

As a child she was too afraid to spend the night at friends' houses, and as a young adult living at home she still could not be alone at night. She needed a parent or a friend to be with her. Veronica's fears drove her to become overly-dependent and negatively affected her self-esteem and self-confidence. Consequently, Veronica's problems spilled into many other areas of her life.

Veronica attributed her problems to a trauma she suffered around the age of five. What she recalled—as a vague sense— was that during a period of several weeks a male intruder entered her bedroom at night and "did things to me." Two memories were prominent: In the first, "I am in my bed, and I feel a beard, mustache, and glasses"; in the second, "I remember waking up and feeling someone doing oral sex on me. I can feel a head of hair." Despite the fear, anxiety, and disgust these two memories evoked as she spoke to me, Veronica continued her exploration and stated that one of her sisters was also molested by this stranger. Furthermore, her sister Jennifer "remembers him doing things to me," she said.

Veronica persisted and recalled the shadow of the intruder

in the doorway, a strong image that evoked dread and terror. The sisters told their mother that a stranger had come into their bedroom, and Veronica told her that he had "touched my butt." However, although Jennifer corroborated Veronica's allegation, their mother did not believe them. The intruder returned repeatedly and continued to molest the two girls. According to Veronica, there was a pattern to his "visits," and the two sisters knew when he would be coming. Once when Veronica sensed that he was coming, she requested to sleep in her parents' bed. However, thinking she was overly dependent and needed to get over her fear, they refused her plea and insisted that she was safe. That night—just as she feared—she was victimized again.

The intruder continued to come to their home until Veronica's father caught him in the house one night and chased him down the street. Although Veronica's father didn't catch the man, it soon became known that the assailant was molesting several little girls in the neighborhood. The police caught him and took him into custody. After that, as is so often the case, no one ever talked about the incident.

As a result of Veronica's horrendous experience, she believed at the time that "I'm not safe," and this belief had affected every aspect of her life since then. Veronica felt unsafe everywhere now. "I'm afraid that there is somebody outside."

We began the EMDR® session with Veronica picking the most upsetting *image* that represented her trauma. She chose the image of a strange man in the shadows in her bedroom. Her *beliefs* that accompanied this image were "I'm not safe" and "I'm powerless." Terror and dread were her attendant *emotions*. Facing me, Veronica reported feeling sick in her stomach and a tightness in her throat. We began the eye movements and Veronica initiated a running commentary of her inner experience.

I have found that some people prefer to talk as they do the eye movements because talking makes them feel more connected to me and helps them keep their attention on their inner experience. Often, instead of using my hand or fingers, I use a light bar that was designed for EMDR® work, but many clients become distracted as they focus on the lights. Describing their experiences helps them to maintain their inward focus. I watch clients carefully and if speaking appears to be intrusive, I check after a set of eye movements to see if they are processing.

As Veronica focused on the terrifying image of the intruder in the shadows, the belief "I am powerless," and the feeling of terror and dread, she began to rapidly process the trauma.

V: I feel fear. I was afraid he'd hurt me. What should I do to get him to leave? (She pauses a long time but continues to move her eyes back and forth.) I remember rolling over in bed a lot. Sometimes it worked, and other times it didn't. (She reports increasing fear and anger, breathes more rapidly, and appears intensely involved in her experience.) I felt so victimized! (Her exclamation is sudden.) I was already dirty. I couldn't save my virginity. Until John (her boyfriend) sex was just sex with no meaning. (She is realizing the effects this molestation had on her self-perception and sexuality. She is increasingly disturbed and visibly upset.) I can't live alone because of this—I can't sleep alone—it would drive me insane. (Her fear of being violated again is too much to endure.)

L: Okay. Close your eyes, take a deep breath, and tell me what is happening now.

V: I feel fear of being victimized—and anger at that sick man (the intruder). I want to see him and tell him what I think of him. He screwed up our lives.

L: Go with that.

V: (She begins another long set of eye movements.) It gave me so much hopelessness when I was so young. (She sounds very sad.) You have to be so sick to do that. (She shifts to anger.) Sex offenders don't deserve to live. I feel like my life is ruined by it. I will always be used, a victim, unable to sleep. He did that to me. He took my courage and strength and sucked it out of me. I lean on others to use their strength because he took mine. (She is realizing further the long-term effects of the abuse.)

L: Close your eyes. What's happening now?

V: I'm afraid I'll never be independent. I have no strength.

L: Think about that.

In the next set of eye movements Veronica shifted to remembering her strengths. She described leaving a potentially physically abusive relationship with a boyfriend and recognized that it took strength to leave him. Here, an interlinking with another memory network occurred, and Veronica was able to access information that had been stored elsewhere. This additional information assisted in changing her previously held belief that she was a helpless victim. Anger, sadness, and frustration that her mother did not believe her when she reported the abuse surfaced.

After another set of eye movements I asked Veronica to tell me what she saw when she recalled her original mental image—that of the intruder lurking in the shadows of her bedroom. In this way I could check to see if the image had changed.

V: (Her voice is assertive and strong.) I can think of a lot of things I could do—scream, kick him, scratch him . . .

L: Go with that.

V: I'd hit him right in his genitalia so hard they wouldn't be functioning anymore. I'd pull out his tongue, cut off every one of his fingers . . . kick him in the face so many times his eyes would be black and blue. He doesn't deserve to have his hands to hurt or his eyes to see again. To make *him* fear would be the best revenge. (She describes tortures for the abuser and gains strength and confidence as she goes.) Make him blind . . . throw things at him, crack him with a bat, taunt him— he can't see what's going to happen—let him feel the fear I had to feel, what he deserves.

I then asked her to return to the original image and tell me what she was experiencing. She continued, newly empowered, with her feelings of anger toward the perpetrator.

V: There are a 1001 things I'd like to do to him. (She is now imagining what she would do to him in the present time—as her adult self. She shifted from child self to adult self spontaneously.)

L: Go with that. (She begins more eye movements.)

V: Kneeing him in the groin, he'd keel over in pain. I want to hit him repeatedly. I see him get handcuffed and thrown into the back of a police car. Go away and rot in hell!

When she returned again to the original image, she reported cheerfully that she didn't feel much fear. "I can think about 1001 things I could do to him mentally and physically. I don't feel vulnerable anymore. As I am now, I could stop it." With a newfound strength she continued, "I was a little kid and I didn't know better. Now I have strength and I could do something." The insights tumbled from her lips unself-consciously. "The things in my life have brought me more strength. I'm not that weak, vulnerable little person any-more."

To check our work and to install this sense of empowerment in her future life, I asked her to imagine going to bed that night. How would she feel? Veronica replied self-assuredly, "I can imagine myself peaceful and safe with my cat curled up next to me. I can see that now." We added eye movements to this peaceful scene, and her sense of strength increased. She left the session light-hearted, self-assured, and secure.

Two weeks later when we met again, Veronica was ecstatic. She bounced into the office and proceeded to tell me about the changes she was experiencing in her life because of the EMDR® work we had done. She said that she was sleeping well and that when she hears creaks or night sounds she goes back to sleep easily. "It's no big deal. No more adrenaline rushes!" The weekend after our session she had gone camp-ing with friends and had "slept great." In the past, her fear had prevented her from camping.

Later on that trip, she had spent the night in a hotel and "slept like a baby." "The EMDR®," she said, "took away the fear." Veronica had also stopped checking the backseat of her car before entering it.

"It doesn't bother me anymore that it happened. Now I know there are a lot of things I could do to him. *I don't feel helpless anymore!*" No longer emotionally charged in the pre-sent, the trauma was now a past event, and Veronica felt cer-tain she could call on her resources of power and strength whenever she needed them.

Veronica also had ceased feeling dependent on her parents and friends. Whereas she had depended on their company if she wanted to go shopping or to a movie, she could do those things alone now. "I know it doesn't sound like a big deal, but I opened my own video account. I thought 'why not?' and even watched a video by myself!"

Six months later I contacted Veronica to see how she was doing and to ask her permission to write about our work together. She was very enthusiastic about sharing the turnabout in her life. She was no longer experiencing sleep problems and could sleep alone—with the lights out—in the house. And, she had even spent a recent weekend alone in the house without any problem. "My cat sleeps on the bed with me and if there were an intruder, she would react in some way which would alert me. For now I just roll over and go back to sleep." Veronica had stopped her bat-toting nightly housechecks after our EMDR® session and never resumed them. "I don't even think someone's watching me anymore. I feel like a normal person. I know there is not a psychotic person at every window. Psychotic people are out there, but not many, and not in my neighborhood."

DONNA'S STORY

Donna, a sweet, soft-spoken woman in her late twenties came into my office and sat quietly on the couch. She was thoughtful, intelligent, and articulate with an unfathomable depth about her that was only hinted at on the surface. We had been working together for several months on issues related to early childhood trauma. She came to this particular session, how-

ever, wanting to work on something that had been bothering
her for several years.

In her second year of college a terrible fire broke out in her
dormitory and killed ten young women. When she was jarred
awake by the blast of the fire alarm, Donna's room was full
of smoke, but it took awhile for the enormity of the danger
to arouse her sleepy mind. Clad only in her nightgown, she
rushed barefoot through the door of her third-floor room and
heard screams that echoed down the hall. Smoke and panic
filled the air as she and her roommate ran for their lives. "I
heard sirens blaring, the last cries of women jumping to their
death, and the screams of my friends calling for help as they
struggled to find a way to escape the smoke and flames. We
watched helpless, shocked . . . stricken with terror." Donna was
living a nightmare from hell.

What most haunted Donna was the image of a naked,
young woman running down the bloody stairs behind her.
Naked and covered with grey ash, the screaming woman was
on fire. She looked like a monster to Donna. Coming up the
stairs back into the burning dorm was another young woman,
her ash-covered face contorted with fear and anguish. This
woman was returning to save her injured roommate whom she
had not been able to carry to safety. Sadly, Donna told me that
the burning woman who was running downstairs behind her
and the roommate of the woman who went back into the
dorm were among the ten women who died in the fire.

"The next day, and for months after, I experienced feelings
of panic, flashbacks, and body rashes. I had nightmares and
felt very isolated from everyone. Others described me as being
hypersensitive and irritable. At the one-year anniversary I ex-

perienced flashback after flashback curled up in my friend Mary's arms. And, years later, I still have symptoms relating to the fire, including panic when I hear a siren, periodic flashbacks, longlasting survivor's guilt for not having done more to save the women, and an inability to talk about it without shaking . . . ten years later!"

This was one of the most horrifying stories I had ever heard. As I listened to Donna recount the devastating events, images filled my mind and fear gripped my heart. Even though several years had elapsed since this terrible event and Donna had worked on it in past therapies, she still experienced intense anxiety whenever she talked about it.

We began the EMDR® with the image of the burning woman running behind Donna and the other woman coming up the stairs. Donna had internalized the beliefs that "I'm not okay, I'm a coward, and I'm an awful, horrible person." She felt extremely guilty for running away from the burning woman who looked like a monster. Donna immediately dropped into her experience of the terrible fire. Her eyes widened and her breathing alternated between rapid and normal. She appeared to be watching a horror movie that gripped her attention. Unlike Veronica, Donna preferred silence during her long series of eye movements and would signal when she wanted a break.

After the first set, she calmly described in a soft voice a little of what she had seen and understood. She said that she had mistakenly believed that she was running away from the woman whom, in Donna's confused state of mind, she saw as a monster. In the processing, Donna realized that *she wasn't running away from the woman. Rather, they were both running from the fire.* This realization dispelled Donna's belief that she was a horrible person. She also realized that there was nothing she could do to save the other women trapped inside the burning building. The woman returning to the dorm to save her roommate had failed initially because the woman was too heavy for her to carry—the woman had been forced to drop her roommate and run for her life. Donna's sense of responsibility vanished during the eye movements, leaving Donna only with the recognition that the fire had been a terrible tragedy.

Donna told me she had revisited the "points of terror"— the traumatic places—and had processed them "as if from a distance" with the eye movements. She informed me that EMDR® enabled her to examine and heal each point of terror without becoming overwhelmed.

When Donna returned again to the original picture to see if it had changed, she reported a dramatic decrease in disturbance. Indeed, she had reprocessed a great deal of the trauma in a very short time. Next, she wanted to revisit the scene and talk to the women who had died. She began a very long set of eye movements—about fifteen minutes.

Deeply confident in her ability to reprocess the disturbing material with EMDR®, she returned to the image of the burning dorm and immediately became intensely involved in her processing. Signs of fear crossed her face, her breathing accelerated—and suddenly, tears trickled down her cheeks. She appeared sad. Soon, her face changed again, this time infused with calmness. When she signaled for me to stop the light bar, she looked at me as if she had just awakened from a dream. She had been in another place, in another time.

Spontaneously, in this session and in her imagination,

Donna had returned to the scene of the tragedy and had created new scenes to bring closure to her experience. With each of the women who had died she expressed her sadness about what had happened and her regret at not being able to save them. Particularly important to Donna was speaking with the woman on fire who was running behind her on the stairs.

"I envisioned talking with the woman who was behind me who had died . . . telling her how sorry I was for not helping her somehow. She embraced me and forgave me as I forgave myself." Donna felt completely at peace now.

When I asked Donna to recall the original scene so that I could assess her movement, she reported that her terror and dread were gone. Matter-of-factly, she reported her sense that the trauma was in the past. Although she still felt sad, Donna believed that she had processed the trauma as far as it would go. However, because I did not believe that she had completed her processing, I asked her to focus on her sadness and engage in yet another set of eye movements. After a few minutes of rapt attention to her inner experience, she signaled me to stop. With a look of awe, she described in detail a spiritual completion to the traumatic event.

During this last set Donna had realized how traumatizing the continued chaos and confusion following the fire had been. No one knew for some time who had died or survived. The tightly-knit community of women was shattered that night for many survivors never returned to the college. There were no good-byes exchanged between the survivors, much less between the victims and survivors. The survivors were like zombies separately trying to cope with something beyond their worst nightmares.

A healing image spontaneously came into Donna's mind

after this realization. She stood in the quadrangle in front of the dorm. All of the women—both survivors and women who had perished—had formed a circle and were holding hands. The fragmented community of women was once again together and felt the union of their company. The dead women looked like "heavenly beings, golden, peaceful, light, and watery." Holding hands, all of the women danced in a circle and prayed. Slowly and silently, the spirits of the ones who had died took leave of the other women and floated up into the sky. Above, they formed their own circle and began to dance joyfully. The women below continued with their earthly lives while the dead women—now spirits and at peace—existed on another plane and were no longer living with the trauma of the fire. The women below were a marked contrast in that they appeared burdened with their everyday lives of seemingly great importance. Donna was at peace and happy with this image and felt a sense of completion. "After the dance, I knew that I would never be haunted by the fire again in my waking or sleeping hours. The fire had finally been purged from my system and was only a harmless memory."

When I called Donna a year later to see how she was doing and to ask if I could write about her experience, she enthusiastically agreed to sharing her story and confirmed that she no longer felt disturbed by sirens and that the fire felt very much in the past. Her anxiety reaction to the anniversary of the fire was gone and the beautiful and peaceful image of the spirits of the dead women dancing joyfully had remained with her. The profoundness of her vision continues to live inside her.

BEV'S STORY

Bev was a strikingly beautiful woman in her early forties with short blond hair and vivid blue eyes. She was an intelligent and articulate business woman who dressed impeccably with a keen eye for detail. Bev came to see me because she had heard from a friend that I used a new, powerful method for relieving the symptoms of trauma.

Bev worked in an office building where a mad gunman had gone on a rampage and massacred people on several of the floors. Secretaries were mercilessly gunned down at their desks without a chance to dive for cover. When Bev came to see me, she was at her wit's end. Even though she had not been in the building at the time of the killings, she was experiencing extreme anxiety and panic at the thought of returning to work. She was ashamed of her anxiety and believed something was wrong with her for feeling so disturbed; after all, she hadn't been in the building at the time of the shootings. The company supported that belief in that the employees who had been in the building were debriefed and offered counseling and those who had not were denied those services.

As Bev talked about this tragedy, she was often overcome with emotion. She trembled and cried. None of the victims had been Bev's close personal friends, but she did business with many of them and enjoyed their casual company. They often chatted about their children or spouses at lunch and coffee breaks, and this friendly exchange created an informal intimacy that permeated the work environment.

Together we explored her reactions to the incident. Horrible images of her coworkers being gunned down as they sat "innocently" at their desks plagued her as they replayed over and over again in her mind. She envisioned expressions of shock and terror on their faces as they were shot to death. In her imagery, blood was splattered everywhere—including on the family photographs displayed on their desks. Bev felt as if she *had* been there. The incessant replaying of this ghastly imagery made her feel as if she were "going crazy."

Bev's strongest irrational belief accompanying this imagery was "I should have been there." She felt tremendously guilty for not being there during the shooting. She had no idea why she felt this way and could make no sense of her feelings.

I believed Bev to be suffering from *vicarious traumatization,* a phenomenon I have seen often in my EMDR® work. Vicarious traumatization develops in several ways, including: reading about or hearing about a trauma, seeing a disturbing movie, seeing or hearing about someone else's traumatic experience—especially if one is exposed to someone's intense emotional response to a traumatic incident, and actually witnessing a traumatic event. I have observed that when one hears about a terrible event, especially if it has touched one personally, one's mind creates an image, emotions, and beliefs about the event. These images live in the body-mind *as if they actually occurred.*

Often these tragic events trigger our memories of earlier traumas. Many of the people suffering from posttraumatic stress disorder after the Oklahoma City bombing were not actually at the bomb site. Nor were they close friends or family members of the victims. Rather, they imagined being in the building and identified with the victims in some way. For example, the bombing stirred up disturbing memories and emotions for many Vietnam veterans who thought they had found a safe haven in Oklahoma. In Bev's case, she knew many of the victims, and the shooting occurred in the building where she worked.

Bev began the EMDR® session by focusing on her image of one of the secretaries innocently sitting at her desk and being shot. Bev's belief was "I should have been there." When she evoked the image, Bev reported feeling terror and sadness, a ten on a one-to-ten rating scale of disturbance. Bev's stomach was upset, her throat constricted, and she felt like screaming. She followed the lights with her eyes and entered directly into the disturbing image. Tears ran down her cheeks, and she gripped a couch pillow tightly across her stomach. After a couple of minutes she appeared less distressed, and I asked her to close her eyes, breathe deeply, and tell me what was happening.

Next, a look of surprise appeared on her face and Bev reported, "I feel like I was there. It's as if I was there. I feel so empathic for those people. It's too horrible a thing to happen to them." I directed her to "go with that," and her gaze again began to follow the lights.

This time she reported, "I blame myself for what happened. I think it's because of my sister being killed, and I still think that it's my fault too. She was helpless and innocent, and it shouldn't have happened." Here, Bev was making a link to an earlier traumatic event that felt similar to her current experience.

Bev, who had acted as mother to her younger sister because their mother was cruel and abusive, was in her early twenties when this teenage sister was using drugs and running away from home. While Bev was away at college, her sister's drug-overdosed body was found in a seedy hotel room of a big city.

"I just don't understand it," Bev continued. "It is so random and unexplained . . . I think I should have done something—I don't know what. I should have been the one to die, not her. She was the good one and I was the bad one. I was supposed to protect her and I didn't do that. I had spent my childhood protecting her from Mother and bad people. All she knew was bad people in her life, and I felt guilty about those bad people."

I suggested to Bev that she allow herself to experience her feeling of guilt while she continued with the next set of eye movements. Afterward she said, "We stuck together because we were all we had. It was harder for her because she was so sensitive. She couldn't defend herself against Mother's cruelty. She was naive and innocent." At this point, Bev was processing information from her childhood that was significant in developing her view of her role in relationships: Bev saw her job as protecting her sister from harm.

The next several sets of eye movements revealed intense anger and hatred for her cruel mother, who had badly abused Bev and her sister. Her sister had suffered tremendously and became emotionally crippled, and Bev blamed her mother for killing Bev's sister. She believed her mother would have to live the rest of her life with the guilt of this death.

During the next set, Bev's anger shifted to sadness. "I wish my sister could be at peace. Now she is free from my mother. Maybe that's why she isn't here. It must be a nice place. Maybe the pain was too much for her."

At this point I began a "cognitive interweave" by using a method of questioning to more proactively link memory networks. I asked, "Could you have saved your sister's life?"

B: No.

L: Go with that and do another set of eye movements.

B: I couldn't save her, but I was supposed to protect her—that was my job. There was nothing I could do. (Realization hits.)

L: Also, there was nothing you could do at your office building to save your friends even if you were there.

B: That's true.

During her next set of eye movements, Bev thought about what she had just said and had a series of insights. She made connections between her family dynamics and her feelings of guilt and responsibility with regard to the shooting.

B: I feel responsible for those people because I felt responsible for my sister. They were innocent victims, like my sister. My sister didn't deserve it, and they didn't either. I can't accept responsibility for those people now. I need my strength for me now. I have to learn what my job is. I'm tired of the responsibility. My mother told me when I was little that it was all my responsibility, and I still believe that to this day.

At this point I asked Bev to return to the image of the office shooting. In a calm, clear voice she reported, "It's better. It's over and done with. I don't see it happening again and again. The image is dimmer and it seems like it is from long ago. There's nothing anyone can do or say about it." Bev assured me she felt no fear or anxiety and that the tension was gone from her body. Nonetheless, we did another set of eye movements while she watched what remained of the image and said the words "It is over."

When I asked her what had transpired during this set, she responded in a voice that was strong and wise, "I feel that it was the time for my sister to go. She was in pain and she wanted peace. I think she sees things happening now and is around in another spirit—she's just in another place and that may not be so bad for her."

Bev came to see me the following week and immediately began to talk about problems she was having with a coworker. I interrupted her and asked how she had found returning to work. She paused momentarily and then surprised me by saying that she had forgotten that it had been a problem for her. She had returned without any residual anxiety. I asked her to bring to mind the disturbing image she had worked on the previous week, and she reported matter-of-factly that it felt "neutral, in perspective, and not a problem." Bev and I continued our work for another year on other issues related to her early childhood abuse, and during that time she remained free of the disturbing images and emotions associated with the shooting.

CHAPTER 5

Healing the Adult Who Suffered as a Child

EMDR® is very successful in healing childhood traumas. These traumas can include physical and/or sexual abuse, grief and loss, medical procedure trauma, accidents, or witnessing violence. Many clients who had experienced limited results with years of traditional talk therapy have been helped at a deeper level—far beyond what was believed possible in the past—by EMDR® therapy.

EMDR® used with adults traumatized as children is usually not short-term therapy, particularly if the trauma entailed severe abuse by a close relative and continued over an extended period of time. EMDR® does, however, *accelerate* the therapy and thus shortens its duration.

As you may recall from Chapter 2, EMDR® is integrated into a whole course of therapy. Thorough history-taking and preparation that includes establishing a good relationship between the therapist and client and explanation of EMDR® are essential before the eye movements and processing begin.

The following are important points with regard to using EMDR® with adults who suffered as children.

- *The child self becomes activated by the eye movements, and the adult client feels like a child.* The client feels as if he or she has a child-sized body and thinks, feels, and perceives things with a child's mind.

- *This child self coexists with the adult self and seemingly occupies a separate and autonomous memory network.* The child self still holds the simple beliefs about him- or herself that accompanied specific traumatic events.

- *Oftentimes life events trigger the child's memory network and cause the adult to act in ways that seem quite irrational.* For instance, the sound of a man's loud, angry voice may cause a strong, powerful woman to feel helpless and frightened in the way she did as a child with her abusive alcoholic father. She may lose contact with the adult knowledge that she can take care of herself now.

- *The child self thinks in simple black-and-white terms: good or bad, right or wrong.* For most people, there are no shades of gray. This is exemplified in negative beliefs like "I'm a bad girl."

- *When the child self has been accessed, the therapist must speak to the child with language and vocabulary he or she can understand.* Simple terms and metaphors that a child can relate to must be used so that the child does not become confused.

- *The therapist often uses interweaves to link the adult and child memory networks when they are not linking automatically with the eye movements.* Interweaves are employed when using the eye movements is not sufficient to keep the client's information flowing to a positive resolution. When the flow is impeded, a client is caught in cognitive or emotional loops and repeats the same thoughts or feelings (or both) over and over again. Interweaving is a proactive EMDR® strategy that jump-starts blocked processing by introducing information from the therapist. The therapist offers statements or images that weave memory networks and associations that the client was unable to connect. Interweaves introduce a new perspective, new information, or information that the client cannot access in his or her present state of mind. Traumatic experiences are often stored in one part of the body-mind and are not affected by more current information. Interweaves bridge separate parts of the client's mind and allow the processing to resume its flow.

An interweave may involve asking the adult self to explain something to the child self, asking the client a question that will elicit an answer from the adult self, and/or educating the child self and adult self about certain issues of which neither has knowledge. These and other methods are described in case examples later in this chapter.

- *Rules, concepts, and negative beliefs about oneself gel during childhood trauma and form the foundation upon which a negatively skewed or distorted personal identity and view of the world are built.* EMDR® is particularly powerful and effective at clearing these early core beliefs which can affect a person for a lifetime.

- *How and what the child perceives is locked into the memory network and constitutes the child's subjective experience, which may be based on a misperception or an interpretation of events.* What may seem innocuous to an adult—such as a dental visit—may be experienced by the child as sadistic torture.

- *Working with adults who suffered as children requires considerable experience and clinical skill on the part of the EMDR® therapist.* This work can challenge even a seasoned therapist because a client delves deeply into the psyche, where fantasy and reality are not clearly delineated and where intense emotional experiences are relived. The therapist must be comfortable working with a client who is in a regressed state, having intense emotional experiences. The therapist must also be adept at returning a client to equilibrium at the end of a session whether or not the targeted experience has cleared. The therapist must have confidence in his or her skill with EMDR®. Furthermore, the therapist must be open-minded about how much healing is possible for someone hurt as a child and allow the client's healing to unfold.

EMDR® with Clients Who Were Physically and/or Sexually Abused as Children

I have found EMDR® to be a very powerful and effective tool for working with clients who were abused as children, and have used it in concert with other therapeutic methods such as guided imagery and relaxation, inner child work, and cognitive therapy. For most people who were abused, this is not brief therapy—especially if the abuse spanned a long period of time and the perpetrator was someone with whom the client was close. But EMDR® does enhance and accelerate the therapeutic process considerably. One woman who had been physically abused as a child and had spent years in talk therapy likened one EMDR® processing session to eight talk therapy sessions. Because of the intensity of the emotional releases many of my trauma clients experience, this work has demanded that I draw upon all of my clinical skills and years of experience.

There are three main phases in the treatment with EMDR®

of adults abused as children: assessment and preparation; processing; and integration and termination. These are discussed below.

BEGINNING PHASE:
ASSESSMENT AND PREPARATION

In the beginning phase the therapist takes a thorough history, gets to know the client, develops rapport, and explains the EMDR® procedure in detail.

Safety is an important issue for clients abused as children. Because their trust was violated and they felt physically threatened, a safe and secure relationship must be developed with the therapist before any trauma processing begins. Weeks, months, or years may elapse before the client feels safe enough to trust the therapist. Trust is critically important because the client must be willing to truthfully disclose what he or she is experiencing during the processing of a traumatic incident. The client does not need to relate all of the details—but enough to let the therapist know that the traumatic material is moving through the client's system.

This trust is also important during the processing of the traumatic memories. Because a client accesses his or her child self during the processing, he or she may lose all contact with his or her adult self and need the therapist to assume the adult self's role and guide the client out of frightening memories.

Such a moment occurred when thirty-four-year-old Melanie, a client I mentioned earlier, mistook me for her perpetrator during a session. Melanie was deeply immersed in a horrific memory of being tied to a bed and molested by two aunts when she was three years old. Suddenly, she looked at me with terror in her eyes as if she thought I was about to hurt her, left her chair, and cringed in a corner, her back to the wall. With a look of wild distrust and fear on her face, she watched me. Her child self had forgotten who I was and now saw me as a perpetrator who was harming her. My adult client had *totally* lost her sense of who I was. Speaking in a calm, caring voice, I walked toward Melanie and reminded her who I was. I told her that I was there to help her clear these old memories that were frightening her from the past. I wanted to connect with her adult self who knew that these memories were from the past even though they *felt* so real in the present.

After a while I finally reassured her, and she returned to her chair. Because Melanie trusted me, she told me what she was seeing: a new horrific scene that seemed so real. Then, she went on to complete the processing and, finally, left the session at peace.

Before beginning EMDR® processing work, part of the preparation entails helping the client establish a "safe place." Clients can imaginally go to this place where they feel totally protected. Sometimes, imagery and light hypnosis help during this preparatory phase. Clients may invite protective and loving allies to accompany them in this place; these inner allies may include past or present real or imaginary figures, inner guides, advisors, and animals. Therapists may call on these resources to begin or close (return a client to a state of equilibrium) EMDR® sessions or to boost a client's confidence when the client is stuck or overwhelmed by too much emotion. The safe place is used to help close down incomplete sessions—a frequent occurrence with clients who were abused.

Melanie had been severely molested as a child between the ages of three and nine. For about a year we had been processing her horrific memories involving sexual abuse and torture when suddenly a lion appeared in her nighttime dreams and daytime images. We discovered that the lion was an important ally for her and she began to summon him whenever she felt overwhelmed or at an impasse during processing—or when she wanted him to protect her child self. Her level of distress would rapidly plummet from ten to zero when she imagined him scaring away the perpetrators. Fiercely protective, her lion was also compassionate and nurturing of the little girl, who felt safe and comforted when she snuggled on his soft, strong back. Melanie would say, "I am safe now," as she did the eye movements with the imagery. The lion also accompanied her outside our sessions! She summoned him before going to sleep at night and would sleep more peacefully.

When the safe place—and allies—have been firmly established, I tell clients that they can always return there, that they know the way. If processing becomes overwhelming, a client can return to that safe place until he or she is ready to resume. The client might also imagine her allies—as well as her adult self—holding her hand or being alongside during the processing of excruciating memories. Thus, a client doesn't feel alone.

When it is time to end a session, whether or not the processing has been complete, I often have a client return to his or her safe place, hold his or her child self, and bask in feeling safe and secure. In that way, a client leaves the session feeling peaceful and safe. I also repeat positive cognitions discovered by the client during the EMDR® processing as well as affirmations I believe will be beneficial.

For example, Frank, a client who had been severely physically and sexually abused by his parents, found it was important to find someone who had loved and protected him. He remembered his grandmother and her loving name for him. I would evoke his memory of her when he became overwhelmed by the abuse memories and had him keep with him a corn cob pipe she used to smoke as a symbol of her. At the end of a session, Frank would imagine her holding him on her large, warm lap; this imagery imbued Frank with love and gave him the strength to face the horror of his past.

MIDDLE PHASE: PROCESSING

The middle phase entails targeting and processing the traumatic memories and begins only when the client feels ready. I believe it is critically important for therapists to be flexible and to accommodate their clients' needs during this difficult, intense, and painful period. Possibly, integrative talk sessions may intersperse EMDR® processing sessions. Clients' needs vary. I saw one woman twice weekly for two years—one ninety-minute EMDR® session followed three days later by a fifty-minute integrative talk session. Some people prefer an uninterrupted sequence of ninety-minute EMDR® sessions, but others opt for doing intensive EMDR® work for several weeks followed by several shorter integrative sessions.

During the middle phase, "looping" is a frequent difficulty when working with adults abused as children. In looping, the client recycles through the same emotions, sensations, images, or thoughts in successive sets and does not process information. Emotional intensity remains unchanged. It seems that because of the intensity of the childhood trauma, adults abused as children have more difficulty accessing their adult selves and consequently require more interaction with the therapist, who helps to link the adult and child memory networks by using interweaves.

One of the first things the EMDR® therapist looks for when a client is looping is a "blocking belief." This is a deeply unconscious belief that blocks processing. "I'm not safe," "It was my fault—therefore I am bad," "I am a victim," and "I have no control/choice" are statements common to adults abused as children. Almost all abuse survivors have blocking beliefs stemming from three main issues: safety, responsibility, and choice. Processing may also become blocked because of unexpressed emotions that have become locked into the body-mind. The following case examples illustrate how interweaves facilitate processing when such blockage occurs.

Safety

Adults who were hurt as children continue to feel unsafe. They may unconsciously believe that they can still be harmed by the perpetrator, even if they *know* he or she is old, disabled, or dead. Not only do they continue to believe that they are not safe, but also their trust in others and themselves is impaired. In such cases, the core belief that must be addressed is, "I cannot trust anyone."

In working with Melanie, I used interweaves frequently because she would become overwhelmed by the intensity of her emotions and begin looping. Melanie often reentered her child self's memory during our work and therein reexperienced the trauma *as the child.* In this state she could not access her adult experience. She would remember everything as the child— the size of her body compared to the perpetrators', thoughts, and feelings. In the child state she did not know that one perpetrator was dead and that the other two were old and crippled; consequently, she was still terrified of the abusers and felt endangered. In one particular session we had been pro-

cessing a very traumatic scene of abuse and sexual molestation, and Melanie was not able to decrease her level of distress.
Gently, I asked her child self what was making her so upset.
She told me that she believed the perpetrator could still hurt
her.

I recognized the necessity of using an interweave here.
Knowing that her uncle was dead I asked, "Where is your
uncle now?" Melanie's *adult* self replied, "He is dead." However, Melanie's child self did not know this fact so I asked her
adult self to take the child to the cemetery to read the name
on the headstone. She did so in her imagination as she moved
her eyes back and forth. Her level of distress, which had been
extremely high, dropped immediately, and Melanie felt calm
and peaceful. She had fully integrated the information that
her abusive uncle was dead and could not hurt her anymore.

Safety was also an issue for Theresa. Paralyzed from the
waist down because of early childhood polio, Theresa had
been sexually abused from the age of two to seven by her father and teenage brother. She came to me because of her marital problems due to her difficulty with intimacy—sexual and
emotional.

At the end of one of our sessions, she was aware that as a
child she "left her body" so her father couldn't hurt her. Her
unconscious belief was that it wasn't safe to be in her body. I
suggested that "it wasn't safe to be in her body then, but it is
now." She agreed and did another set of eye movements. At
the end of that set she exclaimed, "I can feel myself in my
body for the first time! I never knew I wasn't in my body before."

The next week she reported that she felt very different
physically. She realized how detached she had been from body

awareness all of her life—to the extent that she typically went without going to the bathroom or eating all day. After our work, she felt more solid, centered, and assertive in a new way.

Responsibility

Almost all children feel to blame for the abuse they received. They feel responsible for the perpetrator's behavior and feel terribly guilty for what happened. Beliefs such as "I am bad" or "There is something wrong with me" continue into adulthood. "If he's mad, it is because I am bad," one woman told me. This feeling of badness becomes a core belief that undermines one's self-esteem and forms the foundation for one's self-concept. These particular issues about guilt and intrinsic badness appear frequently during the course of EMDR® therapy as a client progresses and targets problems other than the initial problem.

In a session when Theresa and I targeted her feeling responsible for the abuse she'd suffered, she began to loop. We were processing one of the countless occasions when her teenage brother had carried her into the basement of the house and molested her. She feared being caught with her brother doing this to her; she felt terrified of someone seeing her.

T: I feel responsible like I'm bad for doing this.
L: How old are you?
T: Two, three, and four years old.
L: How old was he? (I am trying to help her see that he was much older than she was and was the one responsible—information her adult self knows, but her child self does not.)
T: He was twelve, thirteen, fourteen.

L: Who should know better?

T: He should. (She makes the link between the adult and child memory networks and realizes that her brother was the responsible one.)

L: Think about that. (We add the eye movements here to connect the two memory networks.)

Theresa continues with additional sets of eye movements.

T: I can feel myself sink into my body. He was also a victim of my father. . . . My dad was such a mess and his dad—a whole lineage of victims and perpetrators—it was handed down. That's sad and hopeless, and we're a mess. In relation to my brother and dad, it's sad. (She is recalling that her brother was molested by her father. Her brother's emotional injury then contributed to his abuse of her. She sees a long chain of abusers and victims in her family history.)

L: Who was responsible for your abuse?

T: My brother and dad . . . and I think my mom. Part of me feels like they had no business having kids. It wasn't my fault they were overwhelmed and not getting their needs met.

At the end of the session I asked her what she believed about herself now when she thought back about herself as a child. "I really got a raw deal," she replied. "I was in a situation where people didn't want me, weren't ready for me, didn't appreciate me, and didn't have enough for me. I deserved better than that."

Akin to believing that they are responsible for the abuse, many clients believe that they are "bad" because their bodies experienced pleasure during the abuse. Melanie was one such client.

She couldn't change her belief of "badness" because neither her child or adult memory networks had any information to the contrary. Because the adult also believed the child was "bad," I did an educative cognitive interweave by introducing new information into the whole system.

I spoke to Melanie in simple language that both the child and adult could understand and told her that it was "normal for the body to experience pleasure when it is touched a certain way. Just as when you stub your toe or bump your knee and your body responds with pain, certain kinds of touch make you feel pleasure. What he (the perpetrator) did was wrong, bad. You are *not* bad for your body's natural response." Both the child and the adult needed this information because it was not in the system. As she thought about what I said and continued with her eye movements, her level of distress, which had been very high, immediately dropped.

After the next set of eye movements I asked Melanie what she now believed. "My body responded in a normal way. He was bad for doing what he did to me," she replied. Melanie felt great relief from the guilt and shame associated with the abuse memories and her body's responses to the stimulation. The perpetrator had told her repeatedly that she was bad, and she had internalized this belief and associated it with sexual stimulation. For this reason she felt her sexual response was "bad." The cognitive interweave deprogrammed this negative and very harmful message.

Choice or Control

Finally, the child, who was small and defenseless at the time of the abuse, often develops a sense of being perpetually helpless, a victim forever. He or she didn't have a choice about what happened then and continues to believe unconsciously that he or she does not have a choice in adult life.

Gail's spider phobia distressed her greatly, and she wanted to do EMDR® work with it. She began with her most disturbing memory of an encounter with a spider—that of a large, hairy spider on her bedroom wall a few months earlier. She was so frightened and upset at the time and felt so helpless to deal with it that she went to sleep in another room.

During her first set of eye movements, she focused on her fear of spiders. Immediately, she saw images of her early childhood molestation and experienced distressing physical symptoms that indicated to her that her physical boundaries were being violated. These sensations were probably memories that had been stored in her body and were now being processed during the eye movements. Suddenly, she realized that she was much bigger than the spiders! "I feel bigger than they are, and they seem smaller. I don't feel immobilized, and I don't feel like I have to let them take over anymore." Gail realized that overeating and her weight problem was her attempt to make herself bigger—and that she no longer needed her weight to protect her.

Next, she told me that she felt pressure in her chest, and I knew that she had more to process. She needed to link her small child self and her big and powerful present day adult self, who had many resources to protect her from dangerous people and animals.

"You were much smaller than your father and didn't have control over what he did to you," I said. "Now, you are much bigger and have control over who touches you. And, you are *much* bigger than the spiders—even bigger than your father was bigger than you when you were a child."

Gail did another set of eye movements while thinking about that statement, and it was like a light clicked on inside of her when she connected to this truth. "My psyche is so much bigger than it was when I was a child, and I *can* take care of myself. There's so much support for me. My strength comes from more than my size. It is inner strength now, and I can feel it in my body. I feel my lungs expanding."

After another set of eye movements she reported, "I feel big!" When we returned to the original image of the spider on her wall, she said, "I feel like they're (the spiders) really small. I could do a bunch of things: I could ignore them, knock them off the wall, or kill them . . . but that's too mean!" She was calm and peaceful at the end of the session and felt a sense of inner strength.

Expression of Forbidden Emotion

Many clients who have been abused as children have strong emotions locked deep inside because at the time of the abuse they could not safely express them. The inhibited expression of emotion can manifest as a tightness in the throat or jaw and can block the processing. In EMDR®, clients are encouraged to imagine expressing angry thoughts and feelings in what-ever way arises. Full expression of anger can occur in the imagination and frees blocked energy that has reinforced their feeling of powerlessness. Doing eye movements, clients who have been horribly hurt and shamed tell the perpetrator how they feel about the abuse; when the client fully expresses this anger and rage in the safety of the therapist's office, the client feels empowered and fearless. In many cases, the anger is then cleared from the system and the processing eliminates the desire for revenge or need for actual confrontation.

In my experience using EMDR® with such clients, I have found it unnecessary for the client to confront the alleged perpetrator as part of the healing process. Actual confrontation seems irrelevant to the individual's healing. For many clients, the abuse happened many years previously. Perpetrators may be old and feeble. They may have changed and no longer act in destructive ways. There may be no "proof" that the abuse occurred; a client may lack corroborating evidence. The client may have only the feeling or vague memories that something happened.

With EMDR®, the goal is *not* to recover memories. Rather it is to become free from the limiting beliefs, images, emotions, and behaviors. During eye movements, clients are able to fully heal from the abuse by imaginatively confronting the perpetrator. The client becomes free from the disturbing past and can live fully in the present.

Dana was such a client. Between ages three and twelve, Dana was sexually abused by her father, who molested her in a backyard bomb shelter that, ironically, he had built to protect the family. Dana felt quite helpless. Her tremendous rage at him flared in our EMDR® sessions and, as her eyes moved back and forth, she imagined her child self with a baseball bat, beating her father. Meanwhile, her adult self helped the child by restraining him. Prior to our session, Dana had never had a safe way of venting her rage and so had repressed it—the intensity of her rage shocked her.

She imagined her father's blood and brains all over the walls and floor of the room. She took the bat and went after

her mother also. Her mother had also harmed her, both physically and sexually, and had never protected Dana from her
brutal father. After many sessions of expressing her rage,
Dana felt calm, at peace, and even playful.

After spending several months processing these traumatic
memories with EMDR®, Dana felt so much better that she
went east to visit her parents for the first time in five years
and it was "fine." She was able to be with them in the present
without the baggage from the past. The old feelings of anger
and discomfort weren't there. She wasn't triggered. She had
already confronted them years earlier and had not seen them
for several years. Now empowerment and compassionate de-
tachment had replaced her rage and feeling of helplessness.
She felt comfortable visiting them—although she didn't plan
to do so more than once every year or two.

END PHASE: INTEGRATION AND TERMINATION

After most of the traumatic memories have been cleared
with EMDR®, the flashbacks and nightmares have ceased,
and the client feels free of the disturbing past, the last phase
of treatment begins. Fewer sessions are spent using eye movements. We address broad existential questions such as, "Who
am I now that I am free from the limiting beliefs and terrifying images from the past?" The client has sloughed off his
or her identity as a survivor or victim and must grapple with
who he or she is in the present. As one client said, "The abuse
happened in the past and so did a lot of other things. None of
these things is who I am." Often, spiritual questions and a desire to explore that realm more deeply arise.

During this end phase the therapist may need to educate

and guide a client with gaps in social development. Clients abused as children experience myriad problems relating to the abuse—social inhibition, difficulty trusting others, making friends, interpersonal relationships, and difficulties with employment. All become subjects for the therapeutic work. Referrals to special interest groups, classes at the local community college, and doing volunteer work may help clients enter into social relationships at this time.

It can also be helpful during this phase to review the work that has been done. I tell my clients that we have just put out a major forest fire, and we are now looking for any hot spots that could flare up and cause more damage. Most of the work has already been done, but occasionally a spark may ignite during this time or after they have ended treatment. This is normal and not a problem. In no way does a flare-up indicate that the therapy failed; an issue that was not apparent during earlier treatment may arise. If this occurs, a client can return for a session to clear that disturbance.

This end phase of integration and treatment can last from a few weeks to a year, depending on the client's needs. When clients finally end treatment, I always tell them that they can come back for a "tune-up" if they should ever feel the need or if something new arises.

Into Never-Never Land: The Impact of a Child's Magical Thinking

The case of Kendra demonstrates how an adult's childhood experience of a traumatic event is frozen in time with all of the thoughts, feelings, images, and fantasies she experienced as a child. The adult manifests these frozen childhood traumas in the form of irrational beliefs and behaviors. Typically, children under five exhibit magical thinking, which is believing one's thoughts, actions, and words can make things happen. Young children don't differentiate between fantasy and reality and, therefore, fantasies are locked in their systems in the same way as things that really happened. For instance, a child at this developmental level may take storybook material literally.

The child self's memory network can be so separate from the adult's that despite years of therapy and insight gains regarding one's history and problems, one can still be controlled emotionally by the child's experience, which acts independently and seemingly irrationally.

In Kendra's case, I used interweaves when her child and adult perspectives were not interlinking automatically. As is often necessary with cases of childhood trauma, I drew upon my experience as a child therapist and chose words and concepts that a three-year-old would understand. I tried my best to view the world through a three-year-old's eyes and to understand Kendra's child self's perspective.

Kendra was referred to me by a colleague who had been seeing her in individual therapy intermittently during the past four years. Despite what they agreed was good work, they had reached an impasse and needed a more powerful method to break through the barrier to healing.

An intelligent, highly successful businesswoman in her mid-forties, Kendra was used to handling multimillion dollar grants. However, she was racked with terrible and irrational anxiety. She was depressed, plagued by guilt that she had failed to do something very important, and felt a cloud of doom hanging over her. Kendra was desperate. Nightmares tormented her. Also, she was overwhelmingly fearful of being near windows—and would close and lock them compulsively.

Kendra attributed these feelings to the death of her nineteen-month-old brother Billy when she was three years old. Kendra was very close to Billy, who died suddenly in the middle of the night. Her grief-stricken mother did not tell little Kendra that her baby brother had died until several years later. Instead, Kendra's mother told her that Peter Pan had come through the window and had taken Billy to Never-Never Land where he would be a little boy forever. Instead of comforting her, this explanation terrified Kendra. All Kendra could think of were the pirates and awful dangers in Never-Never Land. To her it was a scary, awful place.

According to the story, Wendy, the big sister, went to Never-Never Land to be a mother to the lost boys and to make life better for them. As Billy's big sister, Kendra believed it was *her* responsibility to go out the window and bring Billy back. But she didn't know how, and she didn't know where to go. As a three-year-old she could barely get up on the window sill. And, to her dismay, she didn't know how to fly. She felt she was a terrible failure. Little Kendra became obsessed with the Peter Pan story and asked her mother to read it to her over and over again.

Yet worse, twenty-four hours after Billy's death, Kendra's mother got rid of everything that was Billy's. Not a photograph remained. It was as if he had never existed. No one ever talked about Billy again. He had disappeared. Then, when Kendra was fifteen, her beloved father died suddenly of a massive heart attack. Once again, her mother immediately removed all traces of the deceased from the house and forbade any conversation about Kendra's father. Furthermore, she moved with the children to another state.

Kendra's symptoms always worsened around the anniversary of Billy's death. In her twenties she would take leaves of absence from her jobs during this time of year and isolate herself. Several years ago Kendra's panic peaked. At the time, her son was nineteen months old. Her anxiety attacks were so severe that she went to the hospital emergency room on three occasions, was claustrophobic, saw a therapist three times a week, and took antianxiety medication.

The year Kendra came to me her symptoms at the anniversary of Billy's death were particularly severe. She had been at a party several miles from home the prior week when she panicked in the middle of the night and felt an irresistible impulse to flee. Immediately, she did so—she didn't even ask for a ride from the friends who had brought her. Rather, she dashed out of the house into the rain and ran the three miles home. Her irrational, dangerous behavior frightened her.

Kendra came to me three times for EMDR® work and wanted to focus solely on the "Peter Pan" trauma. We processed most of her trauma in the following dramatic session.

I asked Kendra to find the most upsetting image from this Peter Pan story, and she replied tearfully in a little girl's voice, "the image of my brother going out the window with some man. I don't know who it is. All I see is his back. No face." In response to asking Kendra what belief went with her picture, she grabbed a couch pillow, clutched it to her chest, and cried out, "I'm not safe." She felt very vulnerable and terrified. The adult self was no longer present. Instead, a terrified three-year-old who was in the middle of a nightmare sat before me.

Combining the image, belief, and emotions, Kendra began long sets of eye movements. She spoke intermittently.

During the first set she said, " My dad left too . . . he seemed fine . . . I don't understand." A few minutes later she looked puzzled and asked, "How could someone get in the window? We were on the sixth floor?" Her child's mind puzzled about this feat. Part of her knew people couldn't fly, yet part of her believed that someone did come through the sixth-floor window and take her brother. "I don't know where it's safe. I don't feel safe anywhere," she told me. After all, if someone could enter through a sixth-floor window and kidnap her brother, how could she be safe anywhere? More sad thoughts ensued. "I want my Daddy back, he would make me feel safe."

I asked her to return to the original image, and she said, "I'm seeing the window. I'm looking out the window. I'm searching, waiting . . . it doesn't make any sense." With the eye movements she immediately began crying. "Wait for me! I was supposed to go too. Aren't you coming back for me?"

She recognized that part of her wanted to go to Never-Never Land to be with Billy and part of her was terrified. Rejection followed. "Why wouldn't they want me? There must be something wrong with me."

After the next set she asked, "Why wasn't I good enough to go? Why didn't they wake me up? My mom was very upset, and she was feeling responsible for what happened so I can't be upset. Since I'm left, my job is to make her happy." I encouraged her to continue thinking about her mother as we continued the eye movements. "It scares me to see her so upset. Somehow I'm supposed to make my mom feel better."

An image of the man in the window lifting Billy up in his arms came to Kendra. "I know my dad took him, but my mom is telling me something else." (The three-year-old is struggling to make sense out of bits and pieces of conflicting information.) More calmly, but still tearful, Kendra said, "I know it's my dad because I can hear him. I know something's wrong, and I know Billy's gone but I don't know what that means. It doesn't make any sense. My dad wouldn't leave with Billy and never bring him back. That's why my mother's story makes sense." Still confused, Kendra continued, "But, the man in the window looks like my father . . . but my dad wouldn't do that—he loves Billy."

Kendra's three-year-old self struggled to make sense out of the conflicting information. The adult information was not interlinking with the child's. Why would her mother lie? It just didn't seem possible that her father would have taken Billy away and never brought him back.

I asked if Kendra could have her adult self explain to the three-year-old what really happened to Billy. Doing eye movements, she spoke in an adult's calm, loving voice to the young child. "Something really sad has happened. Billy was much sicker than we realized, and when we put him to bed last night his cold got really bad. He stopped breathing, and we didn't know it until we went in this morning. We all have a body and a soul. His body is gone, but his soul is still alive. We can't bring him back. We will miss him a lot, and we will all be sad for probably a long time, but you didn't have anything to do with it and no one could have stopped it."

I remembered that Kendra had been very disturbed that there was nothing left as a remembrance of Billy so I asked her to ask the little girl if there was anything of his that she would like to keep as a reminder of him. She questioned the little girl, who thought awhile and then asked if she could have one of his blankets because it "was something to hold on to and smelled like him." She imagined going into his room and getting the blanket as she moved her eyes back and forth.

She sighed. Finally, she had something of his. Then, I asked her child self if she would like to say good-bye to Billy. She wanted to but wanted her dad with her. Moving her eyes back and forth, she imagined holding her dad's hand and going into her brother's room. Billy looked peaceful in his crib—as if he were asleep. Crying, she said, "Good-bye, Billy. I'll miss you a lot, and now I'm all alone."

Afterward, Kendra said that she felt so much better! "I see him as a peaceful baby." More pieces of the puzzle remained, however, so I asked her if she would have her adult self explain to the child why her mother had made up the Peter Pan story. Kendra spoke as if she were her mother and with the eye movements explained, "I didn't want to scare you so I told you a story. The reason I chose Peter Pan was because in that story the lost boys live forever. They don't ever grow up and don't ever die. I thought you could keep him alive at the age he was taken away, and I thought that would comfort you to believe that. It never occurred to me that you would in any way think that someone would take you away or that you or your brother weren't safe . . . or you had any responsibility for either preventing it or bringing him back. I just wanted you to know his soul does live on. I thought it would help you. I didn't want to scare or hurt you."

Suddenly, Kendra shifted back to her adult self. She'd had an insight. "I think my *mom* couldn't face the truth, and that's why she couldn't tell me the truth."

When we returned to the original picture, Kendra said that

she felt much better. "The story doesn't make any sense. *It was just a story.*" The picture now looked like painted cardboard or a shadow; it lacked substance. "My brother died of pneumonia," Kendra informed me, "and I didn't have any closure." What did she believe about herself now? *"I'm as safe as anybody else. The odds of someone coming in through the window are pretty slim."*

Kendra felt much better when she came the next week for her session. She had noticed many changes. She was waking up happy—a new feeling for her. Her nightmares were gone. She also felt joyful and much calmer. "What used to feel raging is feeling peaceful. I feel clearer inside."

Some changes were evident on the home front. She was making her home more welcoming. "I have the energy to take care of it now that I no longer have the inner preoccupation I had before." She noticed that she could now watch television programs that contained tragedy and trauma with her children. "I can watch *Rescue 911* with my kids now without being distressed to the point of tears."

Lastly, Kendra described new inner confidence. She had dealt in a new manner with a difficult situation in her workplace. "I could stand up for myself at work. I stated my position better and clearly and felt very sure of myself. It felt really good."

MEDICAL PROCEDURE TRAUMA IN YOUNG CHILDREN

EMDR® works very well with children who need to heal after traumatic medical experiences and can serve prophylactically in clearing the child's system so memories don't distort and negatively affect adulthood. Many of my adult clients have discovered in the course of EMDR® therapy that as children they had been traumatized by medical procedures. In some cases, clients had sought treatment because they believed they had been physically or sexually abused. In fact, these clients had not been abused in that way. Many of their symptoms and self beliefs resembled those of victims of abuse: difficulties with trust, aversion to sexual intimacy, and fear of not being safe. Young children, lacking the experience and cognitive abilities of older children and adults, may interpret medical procedures as torture or punishment. Many children believe that they are being hurt because they did something wrong and are "bad."

The actual medical procedure does not seem to be significant; rather, how the child interprets and understands that procedure determines how the memory is stored in his or her system. A child who goes to the hospital and is separated from his or her parents, is given injections, undergoes invasive and painful medical procedures, and is examined by impersonal medical personnel will have a very different experience from a child who is treated with kindness, comforted, and talked to in language the child can understand. Common medical procedures like enemas, anesthesia, and injections can be very traumatic. A surprising number of my adult clients have described horrifying childhood experiences of being anesthetized with ether.

The following stories illustrate how medical procedures colored three individuals' lives. In each case, the medical trauma emerged during the course of EMDR® therapy. I think that these stories demonstrate how such experiences contribute to the formation of a child's view of him- or herself and the world.

ROSE'S STORY

When Rose came to see me, I was renting an office that had a small waiting room. For reasons unknown at the time, Rose felt panicky whenever she waited in there. She felt trapped and suffocated.

Apparently, Rose suffered from a lifelong fear of being trapped in small places—a fear encapsulated in a series of nightmares. When I asked her to further describe her fear, all Rose could tell me was, "I'm hot. I'm trapped. I can't breathe. There is a brightness there too. I don't know where I am."

As she focused on the feeling of being trapped in my waiting room, her panic and anxiety increased. Rose was *very* agitated. Soon after the eye movements began she accessed a very young child self as evidenced by a high, soft voice and a young child's simple vocabulary and demeanor. Bit by bit, she described—without recognizing what she was describing—what emerged during several sets of eye movements.

R: I see brightness.

L: Go with that.

R: It's a room and everything is white. It's a big room with people all dressed in white. I'm in something smaller. I can't see it though. I'm trapped . . . something's trapping me. I can't breathe. (She is visibly upset and very agitated.) I'm in a bed laying down, and I'm a little kid. There's something all around me that keeps me trapped there—I can touch it. I don't know what it is. I don't know what has me trapped. (Still upset, she is shredding a tissue in her hands.)

There's some kind of plastic all around the bed—even on the top. People in white can get in at me, but I can't get out. There are other kids in the room, but they're not trapped like I am. I can't breathe. Something hurts in a couple of places— my head and chest, and I'm really hot. I don't know where I am, but they can get at me.

At this point I recognize that she is in a hospital, not in some sadist's torture chamber. She is experiencing the medical personnel as hurting and imprisoning her.

R: A person in a white coat keeps getting at me. I can't get away. He has cold hands. He's saying, "Trust me, I won't hurt you," but he's lying. I want to go home . . . I want to go home. I want my daddy to take me home. He brought me here, and I want him to take me home where it's safe with all my brothers and sisters. I want my own little bedroom with all my sisters.

I saw that the child memory network was not interlinking with the adult's so to facilitate the interlinking I questioned her.

L: Why did your daddy bring you to this place?
R: I went there because I was really sick. I couldn't breathe. I just want that man with the cold hands to go away. I want to get away from him. I want Daddy to come get me.

I asked the adult Rose if she knew where she was. She still didn't know. So, I told her it looked as if she were in an oxygen tent in a hospital and that the people in white were doctors and nurses who were trying to save her life—not trying to hurt her. Only at this point did Rose recall that when she was two years old she had been hospitalized for pneumonia. Now, her memory made sense to her.

The adult Rose explained to little Rose that she was a very sick little girl and those people in white were trying to help her get better. She assured her that her parents loved her very much and would take her home to be with her brothers and sisters soon.

Afterward, Rose felt much calmer. Her panic and agitation were gone. We closed the session with a final set of eye movements during which her adult self reassured the child that she was safe and loved. The session ended with Rose feeling at peace.

MARK'S STORY

Mark was working on many longstanding issues, and in this particular session he wanted to focus on a terrifying dream that had recurred throughout his early childhood; Mark believed this dream was associated with his birth. In the dream, "I'm floating down the stairs in the apartment where we lived when I was a boy. I feel a sense of dread. I float down the stairs; but the stairway is getting narrower and I am being constricted and crushed. It ends with me being thrown out the front door." His thought about the dream was, "I don't want to be here because it's too painful and horrible."

During the first twenty minutes of our session Mark processed terror and pain from his birth. As I tapped on his knees (as I mentioned earlier, this alternate form of stimulation is necessary when eye movements would be difficult), his body convulsed in paroxysms of pain and he sobbed. He breathed rapidly. Moments later, a wave of compassion flooded into Mark and replaced his anguish. He imagined welcoming his baby self lovingly into the world. (Months later, Mark discovered that his birth had been difficult and required the use of forceps.)

Suddenly, while scanning the memory of his birth, Mark was terror-stricken! He sensed something happening in his genitals and related his terror to his circumcision. Immediately, he began reliving the trauma and cried, "They're going to kill me!" His body shook with fright. As I tapped on his knees, he writhed on the couch and screamed in pain. He panted and trembled. I was disturbed seeing him in such agony—he looked as if he were being horribly tortured. Then, a few minutes later, his distress stopped abruptly.

Calmly, Mark said that he felt an "unconscious 're-filing' going on." Mark often had told me that he could feel the processing of incidents happening in his brain. Although this sounds remarkable, clients often report feeling movement and change occurring in their brains; this phenomenon is the physical sensation of the accelerated information processing occurring.

When I resumed the knee tapping, he closed his eyes and began to cry and shake again. "They are going to kill me, they are going to hurt me," he cried. After a few minutes he opened his eyes and calmly said that he felt "tender and raw."

This time I tapped for a shorter time, and he likened his experience to the first time he had felt comfort and healing spreading through him. I tapped some more. He reported a new sense of trust. By the end, Mark felt "great and very relaxed."

I had long suspected that circumcision was traumatic for babies and had elected not to have my two baby boys circumcised because of my concern. Circumcision of baby boys has been known to be medically unnecessary for many years, yet has continued to be routinely performed on millions of infants every year. It was presumed that babies didn't feel the surgery. However, this couldn't be further from the truth. In Mark's case the combination of a very difficult birth experience and a traumatic circumcision experience laid the foundation for lifelong beliefs that the world wasn't safe and that he couldn't trust other people. (Recently, the EMDR® Network Newsletter ran an article about a therapist's work with a male client who uncovered similar trauma.)

JULIANNE'S STORY

Julianne and her husband had been in couples therapy when the therapist, who suspected Julianne had been sexually abused as a child, referred her to me. She was a young, vibrant woman in her late twenties who detested sex with her husband—although she insisted that she loved him very much. Initially, she had enjoyed their sexual relationship, but her feelings changed when his youthful, hairless body became heavier and hairy. Julianne couldn't tolerate him touching her sexually—or kissing her on the mouth. His sexual advances filled her with rage and loathing, and she didn't want him to touch her at all or even to look at her in a sexual way. She confided to me that she would think, "You (her husband) are disgusting and gross, and you should love me enough to know that this (sex) is hurting me."

Julianne couldn't remember any incidents of sexual abuse in her background but recalled hating her dentist, who had terrified and "tortured" her as a preadolescent. Since then, she had always experienced extreme panic and anxiety whenever she went to the dentist.

Using her childhood memories of terror and dental pain, we explored the origins of her extreme aversion to sexual relations with her husband. As a child Julianne frequently visited the dentist because she had many cavities, and he repeatedly gave her shots of Novocain—even when it had no effect. "He'd show me the needle," she described. "The torture tools were there for me to watch. The shots were agony, and the sounds of the drill were terrible."

In our first EMDR® processing session we focused on one particularly upsetting time at the dentist, and Julianne experienced many physical sensations including "vibrating" in her head and the taste of blood running down her throat. Julianne was alone in the room with the dentist and felt unprotected by her mother, who had left her with the "torturer." Julianne did *not* experience the dentist as helping her. She described him as a big, hairy, heavyset man with brown hair, sideburns, and glasses; I was struck by how this description resembled what she had said was such a turnoff with her husband.

"He didn't talk to me, he just did things to me, he tortured me," she cried during the eye movements. Julianne sobbed and said she wanted to get out of there but was trapped. "No one is going to help me so I might as well be resigned to be a victim. *I had to be helpless and be hurt and be good.*"

Julianne was rageful, yet her child self's feeling of helplessness prevented her from expressing it. She gleefully agreed to have her adult self join the child in punishing the dentist. In her imagination—while doing the eye movements, the two of them proceeded to trash the dental office, stab the dentist with his needles, and kill him with his own equipment. Finally, they threw his body out the window . . . along with the box of rubber animals he gave as prizes after his torture treatments!

Afterward, Julianne felt quite relieved. "My body doesn't have to defend itself against the dentist anymore," she told me and quickly associated to her relationship with her husband. "There's no way out of the marriage. I have to keep letting him penetrate me. There was a way out with my boyfriends." I realized that being penetrated by needles in her mouth was linked to penetration by her husband's penis. Her husband, who as a maturing man was becoming heavier and hairier— and thus like the dentist, made Julianne fearful of being hurt and trapped. Prior to marriage, she had been able to leave boyfriends, but with marriage and children escape was much more difficult. "I can't get out of here! The person who could rescue me is the one who's doing it to me, and there's no way out," she cried.

I saw that an interweave was necessary: she needed to disassociate her husband from the dentist. When I asked if she could imagine her husband rescuing the little girl from the dentist, Julianne immediately responded, "I know he would." She envisioned this happening and described the scene as she moved her eyes back and forth. "He came into the office very diplomatically and asked him (dentist) three times to stop it. He told the little girl, 'we're getting out of here,' picked her up, and left. He then pushed a button and exploded the dentist in his office. He told the little girl that he would take her out and buy her a real nice present, not some stupid rubber animals."

Julianne felt "great!" after that and talked about how she could choose whether to make love with her husband. We included the eye movements to install that new understanding. Afterward, she stated firmly, "I don't have to be a victim in sexual relationships."

During a year of subsequent sessions, we worked on other issues as well as the dental matter. Ultimately, we cleared her fear of dentists and, for the first time in her life, she could undergo dental work without panic and anxiety. We never uncovered any evidence of sexual abuse: the dental trauma was the root of her sexual aversion to her husband, and when that trauma had been fully cleared, her passion for him returned.

CHAPTER 6

When All Else Has Failed

EMDR® has been effective with many difficult-to-treat clients such as clients who are not interested in psychologically understanding themselves but who suffer from emotional difficulties; clients who tend to deny that they feel emotions other than "strong" ones, like war veterans, police officers, and emergency service personnel; and clients who have not benefited much from past therapy. Many clients have little or no insight and are not motivated to introspect. Yet, many such clients have benefited tremendously from EMDR®. Some clients simply have desired a quick fix with specific problems and they've satisfactorily resolved those issues in a short period of time. Thus, EMDR® has opened the door to healing for many people who would not have been helped in the past. I have worked with many clients referred to me by other therapists who have reached an impasse in their work with the clients. Using EMDR® as a power tool, I have been able to clear blockages and bring relief to clients who had despaired of healing.

EMDR® processing bypasses clients' defenses and enables them to release emotions never fully experienced. For example, Bernie, a fifty-five-year-old physician, had spent many years in therapy working on the loss of his mother when he was twelve. Although he had been sad, he had been unable to cry and told me that his heart felt as if it had been frozen since her death. A case such as this demonstrates the remarkable power of EMDR® in that despite Bernie's long-term inability to access and release his emotions, he was able to fully release the feelings that had been contained for so long. The *combination* of the EMDR® methods and my experience enabled him to access and integrate memory networks that then stimulated the release of his pent-up emotions.

In his first EMDR® session with me, Bernie relived being in his dying mother's hospital room. As he moved his eyes back and forth, his body contorted spasmodically and he emitted loud, painful-sounding groans as he struggled to contain his grief. His contortions reminded me of a scene from *The Exorcist.* After several sets of eye movements, I sensed that an early belief was preventing him from expressing his grief, so I explored. He responded, *"If I feel this grief, I'll blow apart. It's too much. If I don't face it, then it didn't happen."* Gently, I encouraged him to consider *that* and to move his eyes back and forth. Immediately, the floodgates opened and he sobbed deeply. He realized that, irrationally, he had believed that by not grieving, he could keep his mother alive. EMDR® allowed him to process quickly what had been previously unbearable. As he walked out the door, he turned to me, smiled, and said his heart was thawing for the first time.

The following case histories explore the experience of three clients who would be considered difficult to treat by other therapeutic methods. Two of the individuals had been highly traumatized and had success with EMDR® after getting little or no help from other therapies: Grace had been gang-raped and involved in dental malpractice; John, an emotionally shut-down police officer, had suffered a devastating loss. The third client, Elaine, was a young restaurant manager and had been referred by a managed care company for brief therapy. She had never been in therapy, lacked psychological insight, and suffered from multiple problems, including low self-esteem. EMDR® enabled Elaine to make significant and lasting changes in a short time.

Grace's Story: Recovery from Rape and Dental Trauma

Desperate for relief from her bouts of panic and anxiety, Grace thumbed through the yellow pages and responded to my ad. She sounded overwrought and cried throughout our telephone conversation as she related her plight. Her formerly happy life had become a nightmare!

Grace's dentist had destroyed her teeth by doing unnecessary dental work in order to make money. This dentist, whom she had trusted, ground her healthy teeth to nubs and ruined her bite. As a result, Grace suffered unbearable jaw pain, muscle spasms, vertigo, and ringing in her ears. She spent thousands of dollars and countless hours during the next two years having her teeth capped; when she came to me, she was greatly distressed about the time she had missed with her young children due to her chronic pain and dental appointments . . . and, she was *still* suffering. Nightmares, irritability, anxiety, depression, and panic attacks controlled Grace. After the ten allotted sessions of therapy that her HMO allowed, she had felt no better and was offered medication.

During our conversation I was struck by the intensity of Grace's emotional reaction to the dental trauma and asked if she had experienced any other traumas before this one that in any way *felt* similar. Grace immediately replied that she had been brutally gang-raped in Paris twenty years earlier. The vulnerability, betrayal, and trauma felt similar. We agreed to meet in a few days. To my surprise, none of her previous therapists had asked her about any earlier traumas.

In our first session Grace sketched her family background and recounted the stories of the dental trauma and rape. She had grown up in a middle-class midwestern suburb with happily married parents, two sisters, and a brother. She married after college, had two children, and worked as an elementary school teacher. Grace described her life prior to the dental trauma as happy and fulfilling.

After college graduation, Grace accompanied her mother on a trip to Europe. At one point, Grace traveled to France for a few days on her own. While walking in a Parisian park, she met a "nice" young man from Senegal, who invited her to see his art in his apartment. She hesitated at first but later agreed to go with him. However, as soon as she walked in the door he pushed her onto the bed, and three other Senegalese men appeared. They took turns raping her. Grace was terrified that they were going to kill her but managed to convince the man who brought her that she "liked him the best" and talked him into trusting her. He took her with them when they left to ride the metro to another part of Paris. Somehow, she escaped. However, she didn't tell anyone about the rape until much later because of her profound shame.

Two years prior to coming to me, Grace used a promotional coupon she had received in the mail to visit a new dentist for a teeth-cleaning and examination. Her old dentist had recently retired. The dentist did not find anything wrong with her teeth but asked Grace if she ever had headaches? In response to her telling him that she occasionally had headaches, he told her that her "bad bite" was the culprit and he could perfect her bite in one or two appointments.

His "simple" procedure required several hours of grinding down her molars. As she stood up from the chair, she moved her tongue around and to her horror discovered that formerly healthy teeth felt like flat saucers. Furthermore, she couldn't "find" her bite, and she was in terrible pain. She phoned him the next day and asked for help. Laughing, he told her not to worry and booked another appointment with her. He ground her teeth some more during this visit; she then realized he had no idea what he was doing. She felt he had absolutely no regard for her welfare, and she didn't get any relief for her pain.

Various specialists ascertained her teeth were "a mess" but said they could not help her. Finally, she found a capable dentist who began the long and painful process of correcting the damage. Coincidentally, she met three other people who had been damaged by the same dentist and she decided to take legal action to stop him from harming other innocent people.

In our first EMDR® session I asked Grace to recount the rape, scene by scene, and choose the most disturbing scene as an entry point. She had an excellent memory and detailed what had happened, becoming increasingly anxious and agitated as she delved into this painful incident. She chose the moment when the Senegalese man pushed her onto the bed in his apartment and the other men appeared. "I can remember their black shining bodies next to mine." She said she felt tremendous shame: "I'm so stupid that I am trusting." She felt sick from fear and rated the scene a ten-plus on the scale of disturbance. During this two-hour session, Grace provided a running commentary of her ordeal from beginning to end while she used very long sets of eye movements.

"As soon as I arrived in the room, three other people immediately came in. At that point I was still naive and thought they were his friends. I remember being pushed down on the bed and being startled. Shocked! And I knew I was in real hot water so I tried to get up but got pushed down again. I fought, but he got rough with me and tore my clothes."

Grace described the horror and pain of being raped by each of the men. To survive mentally, she remembered pretending to herself that she liked what was happening. Grace expressed her rage at the perpetrators. "I wanted to spit in his face." She was angry at herself for being so stupid—she noticed that there was no art on the wall at all and that it had been a set-up from the beginning.

Next, Grace remembered the three men going out the door and being alone with the man who lured her there. Choked with emotion, she stammered, *"He looked like he was going to hurt me."*

She described how she had pretended to be another personality; she made believe she was on stage—as if she were watching a play and was in it at the same time. She was terrified that he would kill her if she didn't pretend. She knew that he *could* kill her, dump her body, and no one would ever link the two of them.

"I wanted to get out of there to meet my mother so I acted as though I liked him. I told him it was fun and I liked him the *best*. I went to the front door to say good-bye, and he said in a threatening voice, 'You're not going anywhere.' I said, 'I wouldn't leave without you. I'll take you to get something to eat or drink. Show me Paris.' " Grace hated play-acting and desperately wanted to get out of there. She remembered praying. "I must have been good at it because he believed me. He had a cigarette and he offered me one."

She convinced him to take her out of the apartment. Outside, she knew that she would be safe. She saw a man in a suit who looked fatherly and maneuvered her way next to him in the crowd of people waiting for the metro. "I told him that I needed protection from the man I was with." When they boarded the crowded train, she sat next to the kind man— there was no room for the rapist. At the next metro stop she and the man darted from the train before the rapist realized what had happened. The doors closed before he could exit, and the train pulled away. Safely on the platform, she looked back and saw the rapist's angry face glaring at her. He looked as if he could kill her, Grace recalled. "He knew I had tricked him." She continued her narrative more calmly now, describing how she had purchased a douche at a pharmacy, returned to her hotel room, and cleaned herself for hours.

Although Grace resolved the next day that she would never think about the incident again because she believed she was at fault for trusting a stranger, the past had never disappeared. She never told anyone except her husband about the rape, but his response was also that she should "bury it" because it was in the past. Nevertheless, the past remained.

When we returned to the original picture to check where she was in the processing of the trauma, she reported that she felt "dirty." "Is that what I get for not following what my mother said?" Grace asked as she remembered her mother's concern about Grace traveling alone in Paris. Immediately,

Grace saw a mental image of black vulture-like bodies hovering above her—as if she were dead meat.

For a moment Grace shifted to another channel of associations, this time positive. *"I saved my life."* But, then she remembered looking out the train window at the countryside as she rode to meet her unsuspecting mother in Germany. "I thought I would leave it all behind."

As our session continued, Grace gained many insights. She realized that when she first met the Senegalese man, she had a bad feeling in her gut about going to his apartment but had disregarded her instincts because she *didn't want to hurt his feelings.* "When I meet people, I can't jump into situations that might harm me or the other person. I need to discriminate and deliberate. I can take a stand if I don't want to do something and not worry about whether I'm hurting them or not or pleasing them, and I can feel good about my decision. I can be honest with myself—that will help me in interacting with other people. We can learn from our mistakes and go on from there." Grace also realized that she *had* to cooperate or they would have killed her.

Grace left our session feeling "great" and returned the next week. With tears of joy, she exclaimed that her panic attacks were gone! She was sleeping through the night instead of waking up in panic every two hours.

To check that she was as "cleared out" as she insisted, I asked her to review the rape as if it were a video and report any disturbance. Scene by scene passed until, suddenly, she was angry that she had never reported it nor told anyone.

During the ensuing set of eye movements, she realized that she had been too ashamed to tell, and that it hurt her not to tell. She didn't report it in Paris because she didn't speak

French and feared for her life: she had wanted to escape from there as quickly as possible. Grace felt good talking to me now about the rape and releasing her dreadful secret. "I don't have to have that inside of me. It's healing to tell. It's my right to protect myself and to heal."

Afterward, she metaphorically described her experience of her EMDR® work. After the rape "it had felt like turbulent raging water"; later, the pain and suffering that had rushed through her system had quieted into "a pond full of still water"—calmer, but unconsciously affecting her. After the EMDR® "it felt like the water had evaporated."

The two EMDR® sessions we spent working on her dental trauma were much less charged with emotion than our prior sessions because she had discharged the underlying feelings. Many themes emerged in the dental processing that paralleled those from the rape. She had disregarded her intuition and had allowed the dentist to work on her teeth. She felt tremendously hurt and betrayed by him, who, like the rapist, had taken advantage of her openness and vulnerability. In our sessions, she was angry and outraged at what he had done to her and by the end expressed assertive and positive feelings about herself.

"I feel very good about leaving him before he could do even more damage. I made a smart decision. It took a lot of searching, but I found another dentist I could trust. I got over the loss of trust. I'm not phobic." She exuded a sense of self-confidence, self-esteem, and wisdom.

We met a couple of more times and worked on what remained of the dental trauma. She experienced enormous symptomatic relief. Her self-confidence continued to strengthen and she was able—with much less emotional disturbance—to get through the legal proceedings against the dentist. She vacationed with her family and had the best time since the dental trauma; she told me she felt like her old self again.

John's Story: A Policeman's Healing from a Tragic Loss

John was referred to me by a police psychologist I had met when I had been educating the local police department about the power of EMDR® to heal trauma. These men and women, I thought, are ideal candidates for EMDR®. They frequently experience traumatic incidents and are distressed. These traumatic experiences often cause posttraumatic stress disorder, absence from work, and the need for workman's compensation benefits. Police officers, like war veterans, are often so traumatized by their experiences that they commit suicide. Typically, police officers resist therapy and choose to bottle their emotions, talking about the incident as little as possible in order close the door on the past. EMDR®, unlike other therapies, can work on traumatic incidents like a laser, going in and clearing them in a very short period of time. A lot of time and commitment are not usually necessary for effective EMDR® trauma work.

The referring psychologist was very skeptical of EMDR® and thought it couldn't possibly heal trauma as quickly and effectively as reported but told me maybe he'd think about doing the training someday. His call came a month later: Would I treat a client pro bono to demonstrate that EMDR® works? Apparently, an officer in his department was in crisis.

This officer, John, had recently been at a large family reunion. While there, four family members had been killed in a horrible car accident which also seriously injured his sister. John was terribly depressed, suffered from recurrent nightmares, was not eating, and was "not there." He was guilt-ridden, believing that somehow he could have prevented the accident. The police psychologist had been unable to alleviate John's distress. The psychologist wanted to see if EMDR® "could work a miracle" and help to relieve John's suffering.

I thought John's might be a very difficult case. I did not know him at all and had no idea if EMDR® therapy would be effective with him. Typically, police officers don't make the best psychotherapy candidates. However, I had the police psychologist's assurance that he would continue to see John and that all I had to do was to help clear some of the trauma so that John could function better. Apparently, John was supposed to testify in court in a short time on another case and was in no shape to do so. If EMDR® worked, John would be able to testify. The police psychologist told me that prior to the accident John had been functioning well and that he had a loving wife and stable home situation.

I decided to see John but told the police psychologist I could not make any guarantees. Again I thought, this would be a very difficult case.

The next day when I went into my waiting room to meet John, I was taken aback. He sat completely wooden and expressionless. He stood and walked robotically. He spoke in a monotone. I thought, "Oh no! What have I gotten myself into?" Any emotion seemed to have receded deep inside him.

In my office I asked him to tell me what happened and what he had been experiencing. With an expressionless voice he told me that three weeks ago he had been at a big family reunion with sixty people from all over the country who had come together to celebrate his grandfather's ninetieth birthday. They had all been staying at a campground and having a wonderful time together. He and some cousins had decided to go to a local amusement park, and they invited John's sister, Judy, and some of the others to join them. Judy chose to shop for camping supplies instead with John's aunt and uncle and their two children, fifteen-year-old Lucy and seven-year-old Michael.

There were flashing lights at the intersection where the campgrounds met the main road, but as Judy turned onto the highway she did not see the enormous big rig loaded with oranges barreling down on them. The rig hit the car broadside, immediately killing the two children and their parents. Judy was seriously injured and hospitalized. John was the first to arrive at the hospital and spoke with the highway patrol officer who had made the accident report. As a police officer, John had been at the scenes of many horrible accidents in the past; consequently, although John had not witnessed Judy's accident, he imagined a particularly vivid scene of the accident.

John had been unable to sleep since the accident. He had a recurrent nightmare in which he would helplessly witness the accident from the sidelines. He would see everyone dead and his sister screaming.

John hadn't cried, despite being tormented by grief. He told me that he had not cried since he was a boy because his father once severely beat him for crying and told him never to cry again. John had an ocean of tears locked inside him because of this old admonition.

I explained to John how EMDR® processing worked and

told him that we would begin by working on the nightmare. I also told him that I didn't know if EMDR® would work or not; he said he was ready to try anything.

He described the most distressing parts of the dream as seeing the impact and then seeing everyone dead and his sister screaming. He felt as if there were a load of bricks on his chest and that he couldn't breathe. His thoughts accompanying the image were, "Why are they gone? Why didn't she come with us?" John believed that he was to blame for the accident because he didn't insist that his sister come with him to the amusement park. He felt tremendously guilty.

I asked him to focus on the image, the words "It was my fault," and the body sensations, and I directed him to follow the lights with his eyes.

After a short time I asked what was coming up for him. "I'm scared. I feel how much I love my sister and how I miss Lucy and Michael and my aunt and uncle." John began to sob. I realized that he was too distressed to open his eyes and so I asked his permission to tap on his knees.

John sobbed deeply for several minutes as I tapped on his knees. He was finally releasing his grief. At one point he stopped and said, "I miss everyone, and I can't make them come back."

He continued sobbing during several long sets of tapping. Talking as he processed, he expressed his grief for each of the family members lost and said what he had loved about each one.

When he had stopped crying and looked calmer, I asked John to return to the dream image of the accident: "What comes up for you now?" "I'm yelling for her to stop. I see the truck coming. She doesn't hear me. I see my sister and the others killed. . . . Their heads are limp. It hurts that I can't stop it in my dream." John resumed sobbing.

Gently, I encouraged him to "go with that," and I tapped on his knees again. After a short set he said, "I feel *mad* about not being able to do anything with all of this so-called power and authority. I can't do anything to stop this."

John talked about feeling that as a police officer he had believed that he had more power than he did. Apparently, the whole family looked to him as a source of power and authority.

Since John was not crying anymore, we resumed the eye movements. After a few minutes he closed his eyes and told me he was feeling warm and tired. I asked him to return to the dream and to tell me what came up for him. "The kids look so peaceful." The dream image had completely changed—as had the feelings associated with it. I told him to "go with that," and we did another set of eye movements.

A few minutes later he reported being tired and wanting to go to sleep. When we checked the dream image again, he said, "I see four covered bodies and people standing around. I still see myself sitting by the side of the road."

"How do you feel?" I asked.

"I feel like I'm just an observer."

I saw that he had reprocessed much of the trauma, but I wanted to learn what had shifted for him cognitively. "What do you believe about yourself now?" I asked.

"If I had been more persistent, my sister would have been with me at the amusement park and they wouldn't have been killed."

Because he still carried irrational guilt about the accident,

I decided to question him and challenge his belief. "Was there a reason for you to be persistent with her at the time? Did you have prior knowledge that this accident was going to happen?"

John answered "no" to both questions. Instantly, he realized the irrationality of his belief. I told him to "think about that" and added the eye movements.

John experienced a major perceptual shift at this time and talked as he moved his eyes back and forth. He said that he saw that the kids were happy being with their parents; the kids loved being with their mother and father, and they were having a great time together. Everyone in the car was happy, and he saw them all at peace as a loving family that died together. This luminous vision gave John a profound sense of peace, and his face and body relaxed: the enormous weight on his chest was gone.

John's longstanding belief that he controlled life's events had shifted also. "Life is so much bigger than we are—we only think we are in control," he commented. John's sense of responsibility was apt to be more realistic from now on.

After another set of eye movements, John said that he felt sad and a tad guilty that he didn't get a chance to say goodbye to his aunt and uncle and that he hadn't spent more time with his cousins. I suggested that he imagine saying goodbye and tell each of them what he needed to say. He readily agreed so I resumed tapping on his knees. He sobbed as he imagined seeing each family member and telling them how he loved them and missed them. Tearfully, he bade each person farewell. John held nothing back and these moments were intense.

After several minutes, John stopped crying and looked at me. He appeared tremendously relieved. I felt as if we had been through a profoundly moving experience together.

When he returned to the dream image, it was completely different from the very disturbing image that had plagued him in nightmares. Now, he saw himself as outside the scene and saw his family members together at peace. He was no longer disturbed.

As we closed the session he was totally different from the man who had walked into my office ninety minutes earlier. John was now relaxed, smiling, and talkative—he even joked about his mischievous childhood. He likened his relief to a ton of bricks taken off his chest; he was astounded at what he had released during the session. His guilt and sense of responsibility were gone, leaving him only the normal pain of loss of loved ones and knew time would heal that pain. John gave me a big warm hug as he left.

A few weeks later I called the police psychologist who had referred John to me to see how John was doing since our session. Apparently, John was doing fine; in fact, he had testified in a court proceeding the day after our session. EMDR® had been the needed breakthrough. John's nightmares had ceased and he was sleeping much better.

Recently, I contacted John to see how he was doing and to ask his permission to write about our work. He was happy to hear from me and in a voice filled with emotion he said that the session had helped him *so* much!

"I was able to put some of my worries to rest. Before, I wasn't able to do that because I was taking too much responsibility. It helped me immensely."

After our EMDR® session, his recurrent nightmare was no longer threatening or scary; John understood what was going on. "That one session changed my outlook on the dream—which was a welcome relief."

"I was skeptical coming to you, but I came out a total believer in EMDR®. My mind took off all by itself—I had no control over it. I couldn't believe how physically exhausted I felt after the session—like I'd played ten full-court basketball games. I was drained. My chest felt a lot lighter, like a great weight had been removed."

John benefited from more than simply a shift in his view of himself. "I learned a lot about life after that. I developed a new perspective on life and a different outlook on my work as well. I have more compassion now—my eyes opened a lot more. I try to go out of my way to help everyone I come into contact with."

Indeed, John sounded as if he were doing well despite the sadness he felt as the anniversary of the accident approached. He realized that his sorrow was normal and knew I was available if he wished further help. Even though I had only met John once, and that was a year ago, I felt as if a dear friend were talking to me. He was very open and candid. With much appreciation for each other, we ended our conversation. I was profoundly moved and inspired.

Elaine's Story: Successful, Brief, Life-changing Therapy with a Psychologically Unsophisticated Client

Elaine's story illustrates how EMDR® can work very effectively for some people who aren't usually considered prime candidates for insight-oriented therapy. In only nine sessions, four of which involved EMDR® processing, Elaine experienced major changes in self-confidence and self-worth. She shed her depression and made significant changes in her life.

Elaine was not your usual psychotherapy client. She was very shy, was not psychologically-minded or introspective, wasn't used to talking about her feelings with anyone—much less a total stranger, and had never been in therapy. An attractive woman with a strong stocky build, she reminded me of a farm woman, someone accustomed to working with her hands and being out-of-doors. As it turned out, Elaine's passion was horses: she loved to ride and show horses in the Western tradition.

Elaine was referred to me by her managed care company for brief therapy to focus on work-related stress. She began to cry as she talked about her frustration as manager of a fast-food restaurant. Working in a chaotic job she didn't enjoy, Elaine felt trapped and unhappy. Because of low self-esteem, depression, and minimal self-confidence, she didn't believe she could change her current situation.

"Everybody else is better than me," she said, identifying a deeply held belief that she connected to her low self-esteem. She was the youngest of four children and her closest sibling was a brother three years older. Her siblings teased her a lot and convinced her that they were better than she. Her weight was a particular sore spot for her because she was the only child that was overweight. Her brothers and sisters picked on her mercilessly, taunting her and calling her "fat brat."

In our first EMDR® session we decided to work on the effects of this teasing. One of Elaine's earliest and strongest memories of this teasing was as a five-year-old with her family on vacation in Hawaii. At a hotel swimming pool, her brother called her "fat brat" in front of a boy she didn't know. "The kid was laughing at me too. I couldn't get him to stop." With tears in her eyes, she told me that she felt crushed and humiliated and believed that he was "probably right."

We began the eye movements. Tears ran down her cheeks and she quickly wiped them away as she reprocessed the scene. After maybe twenty-four passes, I asked her what was happening. She said that the picture was fading. However, I asked her to bring up the picture again and to do another short set of eye movements.

This time the picture was so distant that it didn't hurt anymore. I wanted to check her belief about herself now because the processing had seemed to occur very quickly; I needed to know if her cognitive channels were clear.

"What do you believe about the little girl?" I asked.

Elaine responded tearfully, "She probably *is* fat but doesn't deserve to have her brother picking on her and laughing at her."

She did another set of eye movements, but this time she witnessed the picture from a distance. "These other two kids are stupid for making fun of this kid." Objectively, she recognized that her child self had been mistreated and saw that the other kids were wrong for treating her that way. After the next short set of eye movements, the picture no longer bothered her.

Only ten minutes had elapsed. Since we had plenty of time left in our session, I asked her to think of another time her brother had teased her that was disturbing for her.

When she was growing up, she was the youngest in a group of kids who played together on the street. They made fun of her because she couldn't keep up with them due to her small size. In telling the story, she began to cry again and realized that she had believed that "I can't keep up with them. I'm worthless, they are all better than me." It was obvious to both of us that these were the same beliefs that undermined her self-esteem now.

She pictured the group of kids running away from her and thought of the beliefs she had formed then while her eyes moved back and forth. Shortly, I asked her to close her eyes and describe what was happening. Elaine said that she felt removed from the image, "like it's not me." She went on to say that she had flipped through many different instances of being left out and mocked when she was a little girl because she was the youngest.

She did another set of eye movements while she focused on this theme of exclusion. Elaine remembered many more times of being ostracized. "I felt like I wasn't good enough," she cried.

After another short set, Elaine had a revelation. "I let how I think other people see me affect how I see myself." She realized that *she had been judging herself all her life as she thought others judged her.*

By the end of the session Elaine was no longer disturbed by the image of the kids running away. She felt quite removed from it, as if she were viewing the scene from a distance.

"I can see that she (her child self) felt she wasn't good enough because she was smaller and couldn't do the things the older kids could do. I can see it and understand it." At this point, we returned to the image of her brother taunting her at poolside. It no longer bothered her either.

When I saw Elaine the next week, she told me that she felt better already! Her self-esteem had increased after our session. She had realized that being younger than the other kids made it harder for her to do the things they did; she was not inherently inferior to them. Elaine was clear about her goals: she wanted to stop worrying about what others thought of her and be less nervous around them.

We focused on her early childhood beliefs of inferiority in our next three EMDR® sessions, and Elaine particularly paid attention to her sister, four years Elaine's senior, who was very critical of her and whose approval Elaine sought. We began with a very painful memory, one that Elaine associated with the belief that she was worthless.

"I was a little kid, about five or six years old, and I wanted to talk to my sister in her room. She pushed me aside and told me, 'Get away, little kid!' I then went to talk to my brother and he did the same thing. I believed I was worthless."

After a short set of eye movements—about fifty passes, I asked what was coming up for her. She replied that the picture felt more removed. After another round, she said that it still felt removed and was not hurting as much anymore. "I was a lot younger so they were able to treat me like I was less than them, and I believed them." She thought about that while doing another set of eye movements, and said emphatically, "I had believed them, and it was just a kid thing. They were picking on me. I was attempting to get companionship, and they shut me out. It was their problem." At this point, I knew Elaine saw the event from an adult's objective perspective and was no longer identified with the child's perspective.

More insights followed more eye movements. She realized that her siblings' treatment of her had nothing to do with her *worth.* Her hurt diminished and completely disappeared!

When I asked what she believed now, she asserted, "I am worthy of companionship." We did another set of eye movements to fully install this belief with the earlier image, and afterward Elaine thought that her new belief had replaced the incident.

Elaine had moved very quickly with EMDR®, and since we still had half of the fifty-minute session left, we decided to look for other related incidents. Once again teary, Elaine said there was a general feeling that her sister Beth didn't think that Elaine was as good as she was.

She focused on that feeling and added eye movements. In moments she said, "My sister is critical of everyone to this day." Elaine continued with more eye movement sets. "No matter what I do I can't win around Beth." She remembered many of Beth's criticisms. And Elaine saw that she felt guilty for her negative feelings toward her sister. Angrily, she blurted that Beth was probably the source for Elaine's belief that other people were judging her. By this time, our time had run out so we noted where she was and ended the session.

The following week we picked up where we had stopped. Elaine began by focusing on a particularly upsetting memory of Beth's criticism. Elaine had just bought a new truck, which she took great pride in, and showed it to her sister. Beth made fun of it, and Elaine was very hurt.

After a few sets of eye movements, the hurt diminished. Elaine said, "It was her problem, not mine. I can see more clearly it had nothing to do with me. It had to do with her wanting to hurt me. There were so many incidents of her trying to hurt me or my brother to keep her feeling superior."

Elaine was gaining insights about her sister. Once again

Elaine could view the situation objectively. "It is clearer to me that in many instances I was blaming myself and feeling guilty for feeling angry with her." Elaine began to cry. Soon, anger stirred within her. She was mad at Beth for the mistreatment.

She recalled other incidents in which Beth made Elaine feel invalid. Suddenly she realized, "It's not that I'm invalid—it's that she's trying to make herself valid in her own mind. I can recognize that now if I talk with her."

We reinforced that realization with eye movements after which she said confidently, "I feel stronger now. I feel I understand more."

Elaine had insight after insight about her relationship with Beth and how it affected Elaine's self-perception. These were "ah ha!" experiences—as if a light went on inside her mind. I could almost see her mind restructuring her internal view! I could see a big shift in Elaine that transpired during the session. She felt strong, sure of herself, and self-confident. The child's narrow perspective of herself had changed to a broader, more objective adult perspective.

The next week Elaine excitedly told me how much better she was feeling. She worried less about what people were thinking about her and felt more self-confident. She had showed her horse and did the best she had ever done. She felt great!

By the end of our work Elaine had made positive changes in all of the areas we had targeted. Her self-esteem was much better. She was progressing and advancing in her job. In fact, she was doing so well that her boss was offering Elaine new opportunities for advancement. She felt good about her managerial ability and wanted to teach and train—something she would never have considered previously because of her low self-esteem, low self-confidence, and fear of public speaking. Elaine laughed as she spoke. She looked more attractive—she had lightened up!

Six months later I called Elaine to see how she was doing and to ask her permission to write about our work together. She enthusiastically agreed and told me how much she had benefited from our work. Even though the therapy had been brief, it had made a huge difference in the way she felt about herself.

"I'm capable and I'm a good person. My overall image of myself has changed. Now if I want to do something, I know I can."

She had advanced as far as she could within the restaurant business and was looking for work that suited her better. Her personal life had bloomed too, and she had made new friends. She was also working with a horse trainer.

Happily, Elaine told me that her relationship with her sister had changed. "I am able to interact with my sister on a different level now. I don't feel like she is going to attack me. I don't feel her criticizing everything I do. In the past I would have been looking for something critical, but now I don't care. My sister doesn't have the same power anymore. I don't react in the old way. It is now possible to have a good sister relationship."

CHAPTER 7

Freedom from Disturbing Memories

Disturbing memories that plague the mind and body un-
derlie many psychological problems. Memories of life-
threatening incidents, vivid deaths, and childhood abuse may
be suppressed from consciousness but may account for physical symptoms or contemporary attitudes and behaviors. Sometimes, a person can see no more than the image of a beloved
one at the moment of death or in a casket; the person can't recall any happy memories. This chapter describes how EMDR®
processing both clears debilitating memories and restores a
fuller appreciation of one's past.

TRANSFORMATION OF PSYCHOLOGICAL MEMORY TO OBJECTIVE MEMORY

Psychological memory refers to memory that is emotionally
charged, alive in the present, and personal. We expend enormous energy in maintaining our psychological past, which
forms the basis for our personal identity: we believe we *are* our
history.

On the other hand, objective memory is factual, impersonal, and feels *in* the past. Objective memory lacks emotional charge. After EMDR® sessions, clients often report that their old memories, including those of terrible abuse or traumatic loss, no longer feel personal but as if they belong to the past. Commonly, clients report that "it is over," "it is in the past," or "it's like seeing it from above." They no longer feel like they are their histories.

Clearing of Disturbing Memories

Often after a traumatic event, a person is disturbed by a re-play of the trauma in the form of nightmares or flashbacks during the day. These terrible intrusions seem to have a life of their own. Twenty-plus years after the war, Vietnam vet-erans continue to suffer such symptoms. Until the develop-ment of EMDR®, little was available, aside from medication, to relieve the disturbing images from plaguing the minds of vets suffering from the aftermath of traumatic incidents. EMDR® therapy has proved very effective in eliminating flashbacks, nightmares, and intrusive images.

The case of Michelle, whose husband, Marty, committed suicide, illustrates how EMDR® transforms psychological memory to objective memory and clears disturbing memories.

Michelle's Story

Michelle was a beautiful and successful businesswoman in her thirties who had suffered recurrent nightmares, crying spells, and flashbacks since her husband's suicide two years earlier. She desperately wanted to regain the sense of peace she had felt prior to her husband's death. By the time she contacted me, Michelle believed that Marty's jovial exterior hid a dark interior wherein confusion, self-hate, fear, and depression lived. He was expert at making other people happy but was very hard on himself.

Michelle had dearly loved her husband. She described themselves as "soulmates" with a deep, abiding connection. Apparently, Marty was a loving, caring man who brought joy to many people. His great sense of humor always made her laugh.

How could he have done this to himself? How could he have done this to her? Michelle was distraught and wept through our first session as she told me the story of what lead to his irrevocable act of self-destruction.

Marty was an attorney and businessman who wanted "the good life" but could not afford it. Secretly, he borrowed money without telling Michelle, and they lived beyond his means. He sank deeper and deeper into debt. Just as his fiscal mismanagement was about to crash down on him and expose his deception to his wife and friends, he took an overdose of barbiturates. Michelle discovered him, nearly dead, sprawled across their bed when she got home from work. For the next week, he clung to life in a hospital intensive care unit. Comatose and with myriad tubes sticking out of him, this once handsome and vital man was a vegetable. Michelle spent as much time with him as the hospital allowed until Marty died.

We began our initial EMDR® processing session with Michelle focusing on the image that disturbed her most relating to Marty's suicide. "I'm coming around the corner of the ICU, and I see him lying there unconscious and on a ventilator." She thought, "Oh, my God! He is going to die! Oh, my God! What have I done?"

Michelle's deep remorse and feelings of guilt for Marty's death constituted the negative self-statement that was stuck in her body-mind system, causing her great suffering. During her first several sets of eye movements, Michelle sobbed deeply. In her mind she saw the hospital room and Marty attached to all of the machines.

"I feel so much pain and hurt. Why do I have to be strong? Why can't I show I'm hurt? I feel so hurt. I can't believe it's happened. I don't want to believe it's true."

A bit later when I asked her to return to her original image, she said, "I could picture his energy there outside of his body by the foot of the bed. I knew he was there, and I was asking him why he was there and not in his body. I was angry with him for being out of his body. It's not fair! He's peaceful, and I'm in agony." Michelle convulsed in deep sobs of pain.

"I was telling him how much he was making all of us suffer by deciding to stay outside of his body and by not coming back. How could he do that to me when I love him so much? How could he hurt me so much? I'm angry at him for doing that—deciding to stay outside and for putting us through all that. I'm angry at him for not loving us more."

Aloud to Marty she sobbed, "If you loved me more, you wouldn't have done it. If you loved me, you wouldn't have done it! You didn't love me enough to stay around."

Michelle raged. "I hate you for doing this," she screamed. "I hate you for being in my life. I want you to go away. I wish I never met you! Then, I wouldn't have to feel this pain! I want you out of my life forever!" After her tirade, Michelle felt "numb."

Again, we returned to her image of Marty in the ICU. This time Michelle felt sad, but not as intensely as she had at the beginning of our work. She looked at me and said, "It's such a waste. We could have had a magical life together. What am I going to do without him? How can I go through life without him? There's nobody else to go through life with.

"It's a sad situation that occurred because that's what God wants. God must not love me or Marty if he's taking him away. Why is God doing that?"

I directed her to do another set of eye movements. This time she recalled the good times she had shared with Marty. "I remember how funny he was. He used to be so light, and I used to be so light with him. His infectious laughter made everyone laugh." Then she remembered how Marty had seemed depressed and not light and jovial during the last several months. Something had been wrong.

It was nearly time to end the session, and Michelle looked calm. I asked her to return to the original picture.

"He's still in a coma. I'm standing by his feet, but I'm also above him and looking down on both of us. (She is now witnessing the scene objectively.) It's almost as if he's a stranger. I've accepted the condition he's in and am just waiting."

I asked her what she believed now, and she answered that she no longer felt responsible for his death. "I was caught up in circumstances because I knew him. *He* was responsible for his actions." Michelle saw that she was just one part of a much bigger picture. Quite matter-of-factly and in a strong, unwavering voice she said, "It's in the past, it's like I'm reading it in a newspaper—I feel very distant from it."

Michelle's nightmares, flashbacks, and intrusive images ceased after that session. We continued our work together for several months and focused primarily on other issues. Whenever I checked with her regarding images from Marty's death,

she said she felt neutral and distant from them. She had definitely cleared the disturbing images from her mind and was
able to proceed with her life.

ALAN'S STORY

Car accidents often leave a person shaken and unable to
drive with the same confidence. While driving, images from
the accident pop into his or her mind and send adrenaline
surging through the body. Alan's story illustrates how EMDR®
can be very effective in clearing traumatic post-accident images and transforming them to objective memory.

Cruise control set at seventy-five miles per hour, Alan was
speeding along a long stretch of monotonous freeway when
he fell asleep. His shiny, new Chevrolet cut across three lanes
of traffic and jumped the center divider, the accelerator stuck
until the car finally landed upside down. Miraculously, he
wasn't killed.

When he regained consciousness, Alan was disoriented and
in terrible pain. He spent two weeks in the intensive care unit
of the local hospital. Although Alan had nearly fully recov-
ered from his physical injuries when he came to see me, he
was fearful when driving and couldn't make himself drive on
the stretch of freeway where the accident had occurred.

He processed the accident from the beginning to the end—
like a movie—in only one EMDR® processing session, and at
the end he was free of the disturbing images and fear that had
been locked in his mind and body. The next week I asked him
what arose when he brought up the image of the accident, and
he said matter-of-factly, "It now seems unreal. I feel removed
from it. The memory doesn't feel frightening—it feels like
something I read in a book that I am reciting. I am looking at

the picture of the accident, but I don't feel like I'm in it any-more."

Alan is no longer fearful when driving. He also claims that he will never again use cruise control and will be well-rested before driving.

THELMA'S STORY

The death of a child is one of the most emotionally dev-astating losses that a parent can experience. Thelma's beau-tiful, curly blond-haired, blue-eyed son, Timmy, was only six months old when he died from an allergic reaction to the pertussis in a routine DPT shot he had received the day be-fore. At 6:45 A.M. Thelma had heard Timmy thrashing in his crib and found him foaming at the nose and mouth and burning with fever. She and her husband raced with him to the hospital where the nightmare continued throughout the entire day. He came close to dying twice that day and was "coded" each time. Nevertheless, he managed to pull through. However, after the first close call, Thelma and her husband were told that Timmy was brain dead; after the sec-ond crisis, he was blind; and, finally, he lost the grip in his little hands. His little body became cold and, painfully, they decided to disconnect the life supports. Thelma and her hus-band had some time alone with Timmy; they held him, ten-derly kissed him, and said their good-byes. They cried and cried and cried.

Twenty years after Timmy's death, Thelma still felt pain, anguish, the rush of terror she'd felt at the time, and guilt of not being able to save his life. The latter gnawed at her, un-dermining her sense of self-worth. Thelma felt blamed by her husband and unconsciously accepted that blame. Timmy's death had also made her much more protective of her four daughters.

During an intensive and heartrending EMDR® processing session, Thelma relived Timmy's tragic death and the ensuing events. She felt at peace when our session ended.

A year later, Thelma said, "After EMDR®, the pain, terror, and fears are now stored somewhere only as thoughts—like a memory of something that used to be there. The *feelings* are now gone from the memory.

"I go to the cemetery now to place flowers on Timmy's grave, and I feel peace and serenity. I am at peace knowing that I did all I could do. The short six-month life he did have was full of unconditional love. We have our special guardian angel in heaven. My husband frequently told me life wasn't fair after Timmy's death, but EMDR® wonderfully reinforced my optimism about life. Since EMDR®, I no longer feel the need to protect my daughters. I know the right answers to life are inside each of them."

SURFACING OF UNKNOWN MATERIAL

With EMDR®, healing does not depend on memory retrieval; the emphasis is on clearing the disturbing images and limiting beliefs and dysfunctional behaviors that are locked in the body-mind because of past experiences, real or imagined, so the client can live fully and freely in the present. EMDR® sessions focus on clearing blockages—not interpreting their content.

As an EMDR® therapist, I take a client-centered approach to the therapy and attempt to follow, rather than lead, my clients. I refrain from interpretation because any interpretation interferes with my clients' unfolding process of self-discovery and decreases the possibility of creating false impressions. I support my clients in drawing their own conclusions about what content arises during their sessions. It may be impossible to know for certain that a specific memory is true or not, especially if there is no external corroborating evidence.

The imagery and impressions that arise during EMDR® sessions can have various origins. Symbolic representations, including dream imagery from childhood, can seem very real. The image of a woman's father having sex with her that pops into her mind during EMDR® processing does not necessarily mean the deed *actually* happened. As a child she might have been exposed to pornographic magazines, witnessed her parents making love, or just felt uncomfortable around her father because of suggestive language he used in her presence. There are a number of possible explanations, including actual sexual abuse. What we observe is that these feelings and impressions are locked in the body-mind because of *something* the client experienced. What that something *is* can be impossible to determine without outside corroborating evidence.

Many adult clients have been referred to me by other therapists because they believed the clients had been sexually abused as children. Their symptoms pointed to such a history: difficulty with intimacy, lack of trust, aversion to sexual intimacy, and anger toward men. Many of these clients have indeed been abused and the trauma surfaces during our work. However, I have found it interesting that in using EMDR®, despite strong suggestions of possible abuse from the referring therapists, in many cases no imagery or memories of sexual abuse have emerged. In each case the origin of the problem was something other than sexual abuse. You may recall that Julianne in Chapter 5 had been referred by her couples therapist because Julianne's symptoms suggested that she had been sexually abused, but Julianne's problems stemmed from a dental trauma.

CAROL'S STORY

Carol hated sex with her husband and hadn't been intimate with him in more than five years. Her skin crawled if he even accidentally touched her on the arm. Although she loved him very much, she was tremendously angry with him.

Carol's sister, who lived in another state, discovered a few years ago that she had been sexually abused as a child by their father and suggested to Carol that perhaps she too had been victimized. Wondering if that accounted for her marital problem, Carol began therapy, but she and her therapist had reached an impasse. Clearly, Carol's marriage was going to end if she were not able to overcome her aversion to intimacy with her husband. Her sister's therapist referred Carol to me for intensive EMDR® work.

Within several months Carol cleared an enormous amount of fear, rage, and grief associated with her father. He was extremely physically abusive to her during her adolescence and was jealous and obsessively controlling of her behavior.

Carol processed one incident that occurred when she was thirteen. Her father followed her to a park near their home and spied on her from the family station wagon. A neighborhood boy was innocently pushing Carol's swing, and her father stormed up to them, wrenched her from the swing, and beat her in front of her friend, all the while calling Carol humiliating names like whore, slut, and tramp.

During our work, *no* incidents of overt sexual abuse ever arose. Carol's difficulty in relationships with men and intimacy had resulted from her father's violence and jealousy. It seems to me that despite suggestions by therapists or referring parties, clients will reject untruths.

When we ended therapy Carol felt free of the disturbing incidents with her father, and her intimacy with her husband had improved. I referred them to a special workshop focusing on the development of sexual intimacy to help them improve their sexual relationship, and several months later when I spoke with Carol, she told me that her relationship with her husband was wonderful! The anger and aversion toward him were gone as a result of the EMDR®, and the workshop had taught them the skills they needed as a couple to improve their sexual relationship.

DEBRA'S STORY

Sometimes a client's problems are not the result of something that happened to him or her directly. Vicarious traumatization, as I mentioned in Chapter 4, occurs when one is traumatized by imagined participation in a traumatic experience. I have observed that when one hears about a terrible event, especially if it has touched one personally, one's mind creates an image of the event—complete with accompanying emotions and beliefs. These images, emotions, and beliefs exist in the body-mind *as if they actually occurred to them.* Such was the case with Debra.

Debra was experiencing symptoms of posttraumatic stress

disorder. She worked as a crisis worker and received calls from people across the country who needed her calm, life-saving advice. One day Debra got a call from a terrified woman who believed that a frustrated bank employee was driving around with an automatic weapon with the intention of shooting her co-workers in the bank. Debra had successfully handled crisis calls like this in the past.

However, this time she immediately reacted to the stress; she was shaky, frightened, and upset. She felt overwhelmed and unable to handle the current situation. Somehow, she acted on "automatic pilot" and called for the help that diffused the crisis.

But afterward, Debra did not want to return to work. She felt extraordinarily shaken—beyond what she believed fit with the current incident. So she took a few days off from work and came to see me, believing that EMDR® could help her clear what she thought was vicarious traumatization from an incident that occurred ten years earlier.

At that time Debra was a bank employee and was in a building across the street from the bank where she worked when a mad gunman burst into the bank and fatally shot a customer. He took the terrified female bank manager hostage and held a gun to her head for twenty minutes. She managed to regain her cool and talk her way out of the situation. Soon after he released her, the SWAT team began shooting. In the ensuing gun battle four people were killed, including the gunman, and one man was shot and critically injured. This horrific tragedy traumatized everyone who was there.

Debra never heard a gunshot, yet she imagined and "experienced" the whole scene. She targeted this imagining in her EMDR® processing sessions and cleared image after image; she moved through intense feelings of terror, rage, and grief. Some of the experiences that were locked into her system had come directly from the people immediately involved in the trauma. For instance, the bank manager, who had been taken hostage, had described her terrifying experience to Debra, who internalized the intense emotions and imagery as they were described. The intensity of the manager's story so impressed Debra that it was as if it had been *her* experience. She had absorbed the terror of her traumatized coworkers through sheer contact.

In the EMDR® processing, Debra realized that she had internalized their experiences. She felt their terror. She saw blood splattered all over the white bank walls and bodies lying on the floor. Debra processed all of the imagery and emotions as if the actual event had happened to her. "This is their stuff!" she exclaimed, finally. "I can let go of it now." In our few sessions Debra had cleared this vicarious trauma from her system and felt free from the symptoms that her current situation had triggered.

CLIENT REPORTS OF "PAST-LIFE" MEMORIES

Some clients have reported "past-life" memories during EMDR® sessions. These experiences are quite extraordinary and are believed with conviction by the clients. Whether past lives exist or whether the therapist believes in them is not important. The therapy's outcome is not affected. The therapist can treat past-life information like anything else that arises during EMDR® sessions and keep the client moving through the processing until the client arrives at a place of peace and

calm and feels better. In all of my firsthand experience, as well
as cases colleagues have reported to me, the processing of
these past-life experiences reduced troubling symptoms.

Kerry, a fifty-two-year-old writer, was processing a deeply
held belief that she couldn't safely express her thoughts, opin-
ions, and feelings. In her relationships with friends, she found
herself blocked from expressing how she felt about almost
anything. If there was a disagreement about something, she
would go blank or change the subject. She felt powerless and
frustrated. She had difficulty expressing herself and felt an
irrational terror that she did not understand. In the middle of
an EMDR® processing session focused on this issue, Kerry was
overwhelmed by terror. Tears streamed down her face and she
trembled. She was so afraid that she wasn't sure she wanted
to continue with the processing. She didn't know what she was
seeing but knew it was unbearably frightening; she was certain that she was witnessing something that "did not happen
in this lifetime."

For support, she imagined a loving spirit guide holding her
hand as she allowed herself to see what was so terrifying. As
Kerry moved her eyes back and forth for several minutes, she
witnessed the terrifying scene. Crying, shaking, and breathing rapidly, she let the experience pass through her system. At
the end, she calmly told me that she had witnessed a scene
from a past life in which friends of hers had been burned at
the stake for telling the truth. They had all been healers in
early times and had been punished for their wisdom. Kerry
said she had learned then that it wasn't safe to speak her truth.

After this session Kerry was enormously relieved. She has
since spoken in public without anxiety and has been honest

without difficulty in her social interactions. This has been a big change for Kerry.

I cannot know whether what she considered past-life memories were true or not. My opinion is not important; what *is* important is that she cleared the blockages from her system and is now free to express herself.

EMDR® and "False" Memory

A great deal of controversy about so-called "false memory" abounds—partly due to a backlash against overzealous therapists who, based on scant evidence, diagnose child sexual abuse, and partly due to the fury of perpetrators defending themselves by attacking therapists. I have seen clients who were certain they had been sexually abused because their therapists said so. In one case a client even confronted her father as an abuser without having *any* memories that implicated him. She felt he had abused her because her symptoms looked like *something* sexually traumatic had happened and she felt a physical aversion to him. Confronting him did nothing to improve their relationship—he denied that anything had happened. This did not aid in her healing. Instead, it wreaked havoc on the family, alienating everyone from each other.

It is *irresponsible* for therapists to encourage clients to confront or sue their parents unless clients have corroborating evidence of such abuse. Furthermore, I am not convinced that the client's healing depends on such action. Healing is an inner process. I want to emphasize again that it is *essential* that therapists be adequately trained before treating clients. Too often poorly trained therapists or inadequately supervised interns harm clients by leading them to believe that their symptoms mean that they must have been molested by a family member. Certainly, *something* is the cause of someone's disturbing symptoms. But it is important for therapists to withhold judgment and allow the client's process to unfold as the disturbing images and body-sensations work their way out of the client's system. As I stated in Chapter 5, I have *not* found it necessary for clients to confront the perpetrators in order to experience relief from symptoms.

WHOLE MEMORIES AND MEMORY FRAGMENTS

Both whole memories and memory fragments often seem to be locked in separate "compartments" in our body-minds. Images may be stored in one compartment of the mind; body memories may reside in another compartment. I worked with one client who experienced what she felt had been a terrible sexual assault although she lacked any visual memory of such an event. During our session her body jerked, she writhed in agony, and she yelled terrifying blood-curdling screams as if she were being murdered. Despite the intensity of her physical responses, no visual memories arose. However, at the end of the session she felt calm and cleared of the disturbance; she believed that, because of her body sensations and terror, she had processed a gang rape experience.

For other clients, the processing of the body memory opens the door to the separate visual memory and results in an integration of disparate information. EMDR® seems to dissolve the barriers to the integration of information locked in separate memory compartments. For instance, a woman sexually abused as a child but who lacks visual memory of the incident may not know why she is afraid of men, avoids intimacy, can't seem to trust anybody, is sexually inhibited, and wants to scream with rage and terror when her husband touches her in a loving, sexual way. Her *body* remembers, but the body memory is not linked up with the visual memory of the abuse incident. She, and others, deem her reactions "irrational." When EMDR® processing breaks down the intercompartmental barriers, clients integrate images, body sensations, and behaviors that were nonsensical when experienced separately. Clients describe these moments of integration as "puzzle pieces falling into place." The following two examples illustrate how EMDR® facilitates this integration of memory compartments.

EMDR® CLEARS MY FEAR OF RATTLESNAKES

In the spring of 1992 in preparation for my return to Yucca Valley for another yoga/meditation retreat, I had an EMDR® session that focused on my fear of rattlesnakes. During these retreats I love to go for walks in the desert and to climb up on the rocks to a spot where I meditate. I was becoming increasingly apprehensive about the thought of walking alone in the desert for fear of snakes.

I had feared rattlesnakes as long as I could remember. One of the first stories I heard about them was from my mother. She and my father had gone to the Trinity Alps in Northern California on their honeymoon where my great-grandparents had homesteaded a piece of property far from civilization. During their first visit, my great-grandmother, who was a very rugged no-nonsense frontier woman in her seventies, handed my mother a large stick and told her to watch out for rattlesnakes. My mother, a city woman, was terrified and had a difficult time relaxing and enjoying her stay. This story and my mother's fear of these snakes always stayed with me.

From the time I was eight years old my parents had a weekend cabin on twenty acres in the Santa Cruz mountains. I was always afraid of rattlesnakes at this place. There had been several incidents in which we had either seen or heard these snakes. Once I came very close to being bitten by a young snake that emerged from under a rock I had lifted. My brother, sister, and I crouched closer to see if it had a button on its tail. It did! My father then chopped it in half with a shovel as the snake was coiling.

I began the EMDR® processing session with an image of walking in the desert. I felt very anxious. As I moved my eyes back and forth I recalled incidents, both real and imagined, at my father's country property in which there had been encounters with snakes. I was always afraid as a child that I would be bitten at night on the way to the outhouse. I thought about those times. I realized that the snake attacks in my imagination were always sudden and out of the blue.

A new association emerged, accompanied by a rush of anxiety and fear. I was about two or three years old on the lawn in front of my childhood home. I was absorbed in feeling the grass under my feet and smelling the flowers. Suddenly, I was aware of my father angrily looking down at me with his dark, scary eyes that totally terrified me. I felt endangered. My heart beat rapidly, my breathing became shallow and rapid, and I was frozen with fear. After a few minutes of eye movements, I no longer reexperienced these feelings; they had cleared.

I realized that this was not an uncommon experience for me with my father. He would appear out of nowhere and be angry about something I did not understand. In this case, I believe he didn't want anyone walking on his perfectly manicured lawn. Such incidents made my little-girl self leery and afraid. She never knew what would set off his ire. I recalled that throughout my childhood I always tried to be aware of where he was and to put my guard up when he was around me.

My EMDR® therapist directed me back to the original scene with the walk in the desert. Immediately, I thought that snakes couldn't kill me, but I believed my father could have! The little girl was terrified that he had the potential to kill her. Here, I had associated my fear of rattlesnakes and the fear of my father. Now I knew that my father was no longer a danger. That fear was in the distant past.

With the next set of eye movements I said, "I can easily survive a rattlesnake bite." I remembered that few people actually die from rattlesnake bites. My therapist asked what I might do to make myself safer in the desert; certainly, such a concern is important because there *are* rattlesnakes in the desert and a person should take safety precautions. Answering that I could carry a snakebite kit with me and walk carefully and mindfully, I did another set of eye movements.

I realized that what I feared most was a surprise attack. I knew if I were careful, I could decrease my chances of being bitten. For one thing, I wouldn't walk so far alone that I couldn't get help if I needed it. Then, with more eye movements, I imagined walking slowly and mindfully to my meditation spot in the desert. It felt very good to me; my anxiety level at the end of the session was zero.

A few days later in Yucca Valley, I tested our EMDR® work. It was a lovely morning in the desert, the sky was a light blue, the air was cool and refreshing, and the birds were singing. I left my room with a daypack on my back filled with a towel to sit on, my journal, some water, my Swiss army knife, and a snakebite kit. I walked carefully and mindfully watching every step I took. It was like a walking meditation. When I reached the rocky hill to climb to my meditation spot, I again looked carefully before placing my hand or foot anywhere. I felt no fear! It was gone! In the past I used to imagine seeing snakes on different rocks and my heart would race and pump adrenaline through my body. This time, no such thing happened! Nor has it occurred on the many other times I have since gone for desert walks. I do jump out of the way when I hear something rustle nearby—I'm not foolish. But I'm not deterred. I continue to love my desert walks but exercise caution and respect for nature.

In this session my fear of rattlesnakes was linked to my childhood fear of my father and surprise attacks. The child self felt helpless and vulnerable. Previously, I had consciously remembered the different memories, but they had been stored in different "compartments." I had never linked or integrated them. EMDR® work helped me understand my fear and cleared what belonged to the past from my system.

NADINE'S "IRRATIONAL" FEAR OF BEING TRAPPED AND DROWNING

Nadine's case also exemplifies the integration of memory compartments. Nadine suffered from an "irrational" fear of drowning while trapped in a car. Frequent nightmares and intrusive daytime images of her car veering off the road and landing in the water, trapping her inside, plagued her. Terrible panic and anxiety accompanied these images. Nadine couldn't consciously recall any traumatic experiences reminiscent of this imagery, nor did she know anyone who had died in this way.

Nadine began her EMDR® processing session by focusing on the image of being trapped in a submerged car. She focused on her beliefs that accompanied that image—"I'm trapped, I can't breathe, and I can't get out"—and her sense of growing and overwhelming panic.

After her first set of eye movements, the scene immediately changed to a memory from her early childhood. In this scene she and some friends were playing in the lake near her family's home; the children were taking turns diving underwater and coming up under an overturned rowboat. There was enough trapped air to provide breathing space for a short while; and, although the game was a little scary, it was fun. However, during Nadine's turn the game changed from fun to terrifying. When she surfaced beneath the boat, she found little air and was unable to escape from under the boat because the boat had drifted close to shore and had trapped her under it in the shallows. Nadine panicked. Heart racing, her mind whirling, she thought, "I'm trapped and am going to die." She *couldn't* find a way out. Miraculously, before all of the oxygen was depleted, her mind cleared for a moment and she pushed the boat out into deeper water where she could dive, clear the confines of the boat, and resurface.

By the end of the session Nadine had processed that experience and when she imagined being trapped under the boat or entrapped in a submerged car, she was free of panic and anxiety. She now believed that she was resourceful, not helpless. Despite panic, she had found a way to save herself.

Nadine saw how her childhood memory was connected to her present-day fear. As in the case of my rattlesnake fear, hers was not a new memory. Rather, it had been stored in another compartment of her body-mind. Her body remembered the danger of being trapped under water, but other memory components had not been integrated. Nadine left the session with new insight and understanding, free from the fear of water and with a sense of empowerment.

Blocked Pleasant Memories

Often traumatic memories obliterate one's ability to remember less disturbing events, giving a skewed, negatively colored, or narrow view of one's past. For instance, an abused child will likely remember his or her childhood as all bad. As an adult, he or she will have difficulty remembering anything positive about childhood. *After successful EMDR® therapy, clients typically report a fuller recall of their past—both good and bad, happy and sad times.* Clients, much to their surprise, rediscover previously unavailable parts of themselves and are able to report a more complete picture of their past.

This loss of positive memories even happens with recent memories and can be quite disturbing. For example, when a loved one dies, the images associated with the death may be so disturbing that they replace images of the loved one when he or she was alive and well. Consequently, a person might only remember the loved one suffering and dying in a hospital bed or the cold lifeless body lying in a casket. The loss of positive, happy memories after such loss is agonizingly painful. EMDR® can be very effective in clearing the trauma from the loss and restoring a person's access to the full range of memories of the person.

LEANORA'S STORY

Leanora came to my office depressed, as though a dark cloud was hanging over her. She resented being in my office and had come to see me as a last resort. Desperate and afraid of what she might do to herself, she asked me for help.

Her brother Joe, whom she loved very much, had died suddenly of a massive heart attack while driving a truck. In his early thirties, he was robust and full of life. Now, unexpectedly, he was gone. His death left an enormous void in Leanora's life as well as that of the rest of his closely-knit family, which included his wife and two young daughters.

Leanora lacked healthy coping strategies and became depressed. She isolated herself from any social contact. As a teenager she had rejected Catholicism after the sudden death of her beloved two-year-old sister Molly. Leanora found no solace in the words of the priests, who insisted that Molly was with God in Heaven. Molly's was a senseless death which Leanora had felt powerless to prevent.

Leanora was most disturbed that she could not remember what her brother or Molly had looked like when they were alive. Leanora only saw them cold and dead in their coffins. "It doesn't look like Joe," she told me, "but I can't get that image out of my head." Terrifying nightmares woke her frequently and she would lie there in a cold sweat. These nightmares often were of Joe or Molly trapped forever in a box, alone and underground. Sometimes Leanora dreamt she was trapped in a coffin.

We spent many sessions working on Leanora's grief and clearing her trauma. After each session Leanora felt a great deal of relief. During an EMDR® session near the anniversary of Joe's death, she suddenly gasped. Leanora saw a picture of three numbered doors, and the middle door opened to show Joe standing and holding Molly in his arms. They were glowing with the most radiant light Leanora had ever seen, and they were smiling beautifully at her.

Leanora was shocked and frightened—hers was not an ordinary visual image: she could hear and see them and felt they were really there! Leanora was scared and wanted to stop the EMDR® immediately because this experience was too strange for her—far from her ordinary reality. Leanora demanded to know what this meant, and I told her I didn't know. "What did it mean to you?" I asked. "What were they communicating to you?"

"We're happy, and we want you to be happy too," Joe had told Leanora. As Leanora related his words, she was overwhelmed and began crying. Soon she told me that they had disappeared as quickly as they had appeared.

Leanora calmed and told me she knew that Joe and Molly were together someplace—not alone—and that they wanted her to get on with her life. Leanora was deeply moved and appeared at peace. Again, Leanora asked what this vision was. And once again I told her that I didn't know but that she should honor the experience and see how it affected her. "Let the experience speak to you and touch you," I encouraged.

When I next saw Leanora she told me that when she thought about her brother and sister, Leanora felt a sense of deep peace rather than agonizing grief. She now *knew* that they were okay and not alone. Leanora now believed that death is not the end of life, but rather some kind of a transition. "I still miss them terribly, and I know I always will. But I feel differently toward their 'deaths' for I know they are alive and happy somewhere. And since they are together, then when I die I'll see them again."

Two years have passed since Leanora's treatment ended. She continues to be at peace with these losses, and she has *regained a full range of memories of both Joe and Molly. The haunting images are gone.* Leanora still misses them but is no longer incapacitated with grief around holidays or their birthdays. Her survivor guilt is gone and she feels good about living a full and happy life.

CHAPTER 8

Transforming Beliefs and Behaviors

Traumatic events often cause a person to develop harmful beliefs and behavior patterns. This chapter shows how EMDR® processing opens clients to understanding and insights that allow them to cast off these destructive tendencies. Healthier and more realistic statements can replace such beliefs as "I am helpless," "I am bad," or "I am unlovable." Undesirable behavior patterns, ranging from the self-limiting to the extremely destructive, can be completely eliminated. Lives can change dramatically!

SUSAN'S STORY: FROM LOW PROFESSIONAL SELF-ESTEEM TO SELF-EMPOWERMENT

Susan was a wise, experienced psychotherapist in her mid-fifties. Introspective and insightful, Susan had personally spent many years in different types of therapy and had a long-term meditation practice. Despite her rich background of self-inquiry, Susan felt seriously blocked professionally. Susan was well-regarded among her peers and had a full and successful psychotherapy practice, but she wanted to expand beyond the walls of her office and share what she knew in a broader capacity. She wanted to teach graduate students, conduct workshops, and provide clinical supervision, but deep-seated negative self-concepts inhibited her from publicly expressing her years of knowledge and wisdom.

In our first session Susan said, *"I'm afraid of going blank in front of a large group when I'm speaking. I'm afraid my mind won't work. . . . I don't believe I have anything valuable to say."* This irrational blockage prevented her from expressing herself creatively, and Susan was quite disturbed. She hoped that EMDR® would succeed where other methods had failed.

Susan was an only child of Jewish European immigrant parents. Her mother was a loving, giving woman who was chronically depressed because of the many losses she had suffered and who impressed Susan with the message that "a woman's duty is to take care of men." On the other hand, Susan's father was angry and critical and had strong left-wing ideological beliefs, which he harshly imposed on Susan.

Susan described a very disturbing time in early adulthood that she believed was related to her professional blockage. It was during the free-love days of the sixties, a time when there was little consciousness about the importance of professional boundaries and the potential harm in sexual relationships between students and teachers. Susan, who was in her twenties, became sexually involved with two of her supervisors at a prestigious psychotherapy institute. Both men were old enough to be her father, and she looked to them as mentors. Everything seemed fine—until she found she was pregnant. Neither man would take responsibility. Their view—which she shared—was that she was at fault for the pregnancy and so she shouldn't expect help.

The situation became even more complicated when, as well as being supervised by them, she began working for them in a clinic. When the clinic's profit declined, they reduced her salary. Financially dependent on them, Susan was in a bind. They never asked how she was doing, nor did they offer her any assistance. They didn't even acknowledge that she was pregnant. Rather, they acted as if they were doing her a favor by letting her work for them.

This sexual misconduct on the part of her supervisors was a gross abuse of power and was psychologically damaging to Susan. Sexual behavior between therapists and their patients or supervisees is unethical behavior and grounds for the revocation of psychotherapy licenses. Susan felt so much shame, humiliation, and rejection from this experience that she dropped out of the institute. Because her father rejected her as a shame to the family, no help was available from her parents. She had no one to whom she could turn. Relying on her inner strength and resolve, she struggled for years to provide for herself and her daughter. Although Susan survived—and later thrived—the emotional toll from this experience affected her professional self-esteem and her relationships with men.

Susan began the first EMDR® processing session by describing again the most disturbing memory related to the feeling of powerlessness and inability to speak up for herself, the memory of being with the two supervisors/lovers who had no thought of helping her with the pregnancy. As she talked, she became increasingly upset.

She imagined being visibly pregnant and in the clinic with the two men who were trying to reduce her hourly wage by ten dollars. The negative belief was "I'm pregnant, I'm in this situation, and it's my responsibility. I can't expect any help from anyone else."

She stated the positive self-statement that she hoped would be true at the end of the session: "I'm pregnant, and the three of us are all participating in it." She refined this further: "We're all responsible, and I had a right to ask for help." She rated the latter statement as two on a scale from one to seven, seven being totally true. In other words, the statement didn't feel very true to Susan. Clearly, she felt unable to ask for the help she needed to survive alone with a baby. Susan felt "scared, shrinking, collapsing inside" when she viewed her image and felt alone and upset when she thought about this time.

Susan began the eye movements, and insights and body sensations passed through her. She reported that from an outside perspective she viewed herself as a normal-sized adult, but she *felt* herself to be small—as if she were a child.

Susan jumped back in time to a disturbing childhood experience. "I see my father. He is very big, and I'm little. He's tearing up my Halloween costume. . . . He's raging and tearing up this thing that I'm so proud of. Inside I'm thinking, 'I hate you!' I can't stop him!" Susan had saved her allowance money to buy the costume and, in total disregard for Susan's feelings, her father destroyed it because it clashed with his ideological beliefs.

In the next set of eye movements, Susan expressed her hurt and anger at her father. Through her tears she yelled, "Stop it! You're hurting me!" Then as if she were entreating someone else nearby, she hollered, "Help me!" Finally, Susan's rage and hurt were gone.

Calmly, Susan next saw an image of her father before he

died at eighty-five years old. He looked pathetic: lonely, senile, and broken. She realized that he was alone because of how he treated people; he had created a situation where he was doomed to die in that state. He had always been impossible to talk to. He could never understand how she felt. She realized that growing up in her family, because of his violence, she couldn't safely express her feelings. Consequently, Susan didn't learn how to care for herself or express her needs and feelings.

In her next set of eye movements, Susan returned to the original picture and focused on one of the male supervisors. She now had a new perspective.

"I see him as totally in denial. He is scared, and this (ignoring that he might be the father of her unborn child and that she needed help) is how he behaves when he's scared. I see myself as powerful. He's afraid . . . and I don't see my own power.

"I see my mother, the 'servant,' put up with shit and my father, an impossible man. She was beaten down. She didn't teach me how to take care of myself with men. My mother says she is sorry she wasn't able to teach me—no one taught her either. She didn't know any other way. You just do it all by yourself and don't ask for help."

By this time, Susan was cognizant now of the legacy— "Don't ask for help!"—passed down through generations of women in her family, and her outlook changed. She thought of many things she could have done in her situation—applying what she knew *now* to the situation *then*. She was connecting two memory networks: her young adult self and her competent adult.

She sounded newly empowered. "I see myself walking out of the room and finding a powerful woman therapist outside that situation. I call some friends and say, 'I'm pregnant,' and I tell the truth. I have to decide how I'm going to get help. I bring a complaint in front of the licensing board so they (the two supervisors) won't take advantage of anyone else. They were my teachers and psychotherapists. They should have known better."

Next, Susan imagined making the two supervisors acknowledge responsibility for their abuse of power. She was supported in her stand by sympathetic friends. "This is about getting conscious that harm has been done," she stated firmly.

At the session's end, when we returned to the original picture, Susan realized, "I have other choices; I don't have to let them manipulate me. I can remove myself from a situation in which I don't feel safe."

Originally, she felt powerless when in the room with her two supervisors/lovers. They were older, experienced at rationalization and manipulation, and in positions of authority over her.

"I don't have to stay there and try to defend myself," she told me. "With my father I couldn't leave and get help. *I have a right to ask for help.*"

When she raised the image next, a new belief replaced the old one: "If I need help, I can ask for it." This new belief felt totally true. Along with eye movements, she repeated that statement and continued, "We were all responsible. They were responsible for having sex with me. They were the ones who should have said 'no'—they should have known that it was an abuse of their power." Our session ended. Susan was tired, but no longer disturbed and upset.

She looked vibrant and refreshed when she came for her next appointment the following week and said that she had turned a corner: she had released the past. She had forgiven her supervisors/lovers and had no longer regretted her actions for she understood them in context.

This week we focused on the damage to her sexuality caused by her supervisors' abuse. For ten years after the birth of her daughter, Susan protected herself with celibacy. Later she was very cautious and protective of her sexuality. She believed, "If I get close to someone, I'll be rejected. They will use me. I'm not attractive."

With EMDR® she processed through layer after layer of past rejection experiences regarding men and, as the session progressed, Susan more fully connected to what she felt to be true presently. Many insights emerged.

Assertively, she stated, "I learned to not trust because I got hurt, but I can follow my heart now. I can take care of myself in relationships. It's okay to be vulnerable now because I can trust my feelings; I can talk about what I feel and my truth. I can open and close when I need to—both are important."

After the final set of eye movements she laughed. "I need to be fully alive and who I am." She saw herself dancing with joy. "I'm connected to myself, full and alive. I'm a full-bodied woman." I joined in her laughter and delighted in her joy and exuberance.

Soon after, Susan began teaching in a psychotherapy internship program and *had no problem with her work*. She had begun therapy to clear the belief "I have nothing to say" and it was no longer an issue for her.

In our last EMDR® processing session, we focused on the area of creative expression. Most of our work had been completed in the first two EMDR® processing sessions and this last one was a kind of fine-tuning. Susan left this session trusting that her creativity would direct her and she could nurture it. She felt that she had accomplished what she had come to see me for in those three sessions and would call me in the future if she had more work to do.

A year later I called Susan to see how she was doing and to ask her permission to tell her story. She was doing wonderfully! She was teaching, doing clinical supervision, and leading consultation groups. She felt confident about stepping out into the world and being a leader in the community. She was no longer afraid to speak in public and enjoyed the respect and caring of her peers. Her daughter's father had died recently, and she had been able to complete things with him before he died. The anger, hurt, and bitterness of his betrayal were gone and she felt at peace.

LEILA'S STORY: FROM LIFE WITHOUT OPTIONS TO WHICH IS BEST FOR ME?

Leila came to see me in a panic: her eight-year-old marriage was ending and she faced finding a job and supporting herself. She covered her feelings of terror and inadequacy with cool sophistication and intelligence. An attractive thirty-year-old East Indian from Trinidad, Leila had lived in the United States for the past eleven years. Although her intellectual beliefs were not akin to her family's or culture's, she was emotionally controlled by the beliefs they had passed to her.

Leila was terrified she wouldn't be able to survive on her own even though she had always worked in the past. In fact, for the last two years she and her husband had been house parents for a group of emotionally disturbed adolescents. Leila and her husband planned to quit their house parenting job, separate, and move. Leila would lose her marriage, job, and home all at one time.

When I first saw Leila, she was so paralyzed by fear that she was not even in the initial stage of job-seeking—and time was running out. First of all, Leila didn't know what she wanted to do; second, she believed, "I'm not smart enough."

Leila was the youngest of four children in a poor family. Few people in Trinidad are educated, and her parents were no exception. The island life was simple, unhurried, and close to nature.

As a child, Leila was often sick with asthma. Her mother became extremely controlling and overprotective; she did not allow Leila to play with other children, swim, ride a bicycle, or to go barefoot. Forced to follow her mother around all day, bored to tears, Leila felt like a prisoner. She would watch longingly out the window at the other children playing and laughing. Leila's adolescence continued to reflect the same restriction and isolation because Leila's mother, a born-again Christian since Leila was seven years old, valued Leila's being a "good girl" and did not allow Leila to date or talk to boys.

Leila found school painful and humiliating. The children were all ranked one to thirty, and everyone's ranking was known. She missed a lot of school because of the asthma and so did not rank very high. Due to her absences, Leila didn't know some of the basic information that everyone else knew. If a child did not understand something in class, he or she was hit in front of the other children. Before long, Leila began to believe that she was stupid.

The repeated humiliation in school and the cultural values that girls were insignificant and that it was not right for them to be smart weighed upon Leila. She felt intellectually inadequate and thus unable to be successful because she was a girl.

As we prepared for her first EMDR® processing session we explored her feelings of inadequacy. She feared that her peers would refer to something she would not understand that would indicate her lack of intelligence. She cited the instance when she was playing Trivial Pursuit with a group of friends at a party and didn't know the answers to the questions. She felt humiliated at not knowing although everyone else seemed to be unperturbed when they missed a question.

To begin, Leila focused on a classroom experience she had when she was eleven or twelve years old. At the time, she didn't understand what nouns, verbs, and adverbs were. The teacher, whom Leila described as "excellent and harsh," told her, "You should get this. You're stupid if you don't get it." Leila felt humiliated. Her stomach was tense and her face was ablaze.

Soon Leila felt "empty inside and tense." Nausea and sadness followed. Leila was distracted and realized she was imagining playing outside. "I'm not having any fun because I'm supposed to be working," she said. "I feel guilty. At school I should be learning, but it's the only time I have to be social. (Remember, her mother kept Leila indoors, away from the other children after school and on the weekends.) I feel guilt about that—I didn't get the education I could have."

She began to cry. Soon, she was sobbing loudly. "I didn't study because I wanted to play. Why was I going to school? I never saw the point. Because I didn't focus on school, I got poor grades. Then I was humiliated. I didn't want to go to school because I was doing badly. My mother humiliated me too. I remember feeling so terrible I wanted to grab a knife and end my life. Because of my bad report card my mother hit me two times with a belt in front of everyone."

The next set of eye movements brought more scenes of humiliation to Leila's mind. Another time when she received a poor report card, her father compared her negatively to another girl. From then on Leila hid her report cards from her father. Leila stopped crying after another set of eye movements and no longer felt humiliated. In fact, she remembered a time when she talked confidently about college to her sister.

When I asked Leila to retrieve her original image, she was unable to do so. Instead, she remembered being chosen by her teacher to study for a special high school qualification examination! New information came to her mind. Despite her poor grades due to illness and lack of focus in school, her teacher recognized Leila's intellectual potential. Even though no one in her family had ever passed this exam, Leila studied hard, did well on the exam, and went on to high school. This was a separate memory network having to do with successes that was now being integrated or linked with the memoy network having to do with failure.

As she mused on that memory and continued with the eye movements, her stomach began to tingle with excitement. "I feel the support I got from my brother and others in preparing for the exam," she said jubilantly.

What did she believe now? Leila answered, "If I prepare I can achieve it." The session ended on a positive and strong note.

By her next session, a lot had changed. When we checked back with the classroom humiliation scene, Leila said, "I'm a social being. Social interactions at school were important to me. When I was humiliated at school because of not doing well, I'd stay home sick. There, I'd get a lot of attention from my family. I don't feel the pain that I felt then when I bring up that scene now. I see more of the positive times. *I see the final exam when I was successful now, and feel it in my heart. When I paid attention, the information went in and I learned it. I have the capacity to get it.*" Leila had replaced her old negative image and belief with a positive image and belief that felt totally true to her.

In response to my request, she scanned her life for places when she felt stupid. However, no specific images arose. So, I asked her to focus on the belief "I'm not smart enough" and to begin the eye movements.

Immediately, she feared that she couldn't take care of herself. She felt overwhelmed and wanted to "check out." "I get tired and want to sleep. I get started and sabotage myself. I have no safety net with my husband gone." I observed that these feelings seemed related to the paralysis she was experiencing in beginning to look for work.

A number of "shoulds" ensued. "I shouldn't need to ask for help. I should be able to do it. I shouldn't depend on anyone." Leila was very hard on herself. Nevertheless, she realized, "I want to be taken care of."

During the next set she cried, "I don't deserve to be taken care of," and proceeded to process this belief during the next several sets. She felt undeserving because she was a woman. Then Leila thought of how she had both financially and emotionally supported the men in her relationships. Ah ha! She remembered her mother repeatedly telling Leila throughout her childhood that she was selfish. Ah ha! Suddenly, Leila realized she had overcompensated for being selfish by being self-sacrificing in relationships.

She remembered her father as a truly selfless giver to the community, a man loved and admired by many. He gave from his heart, not from ideology. Leila's mother envied him; her giving was tainted with a saccharine holiness that stemmed from beliefs about what one should do to be righteous. Her mother valued self-sacrifice because of her religious views.

Leila remarked, "I feel blessed when I can give. I don't want to do it as a role of self-sacrifice." She asserted, "I can take care of myself *and* give to others."

Although Leila's sadness had decreased, she was very anxious in our next session. Her last day at work was nearing and she would lose her home soon. Yet, she had still not prepared to find work. So, we talked about what she wanted to do and how much money she wanted to earn. Leila was well-trained in the food service industry and had a strong interest in catering.

As we focused on the discrete steps necessary to promote such a business, I noticed that Leila was excellent at enumerating the tasks she needed to do. But, she spewed a barrage of limiting beliefs—"I'm not good enough . . . not smart enough . . . no one will want my services . . . I will start the business and screw it up."

Instead of addressing the negative beliefs, I asked her to move her eyes back and forth and imagine doing the work she wanted to do. I wanted to reinforce her positive vision of work she loved. Minutes later, she said, "It feels good to me. The work is flexible and I can work independently—and, my creative needs will be met. I see a very successful business. It feels honest and clean."

I directed her "to take that positive feeling about doing the work you want to do and imagine doing what you need to do to promote yourself." I wanted to see if she could bring her resources into future action. After a few minutes of doing more eye movements, Leila felt humiliated again. "If someone asked me a question I didn't know the answer to, I'd feel humiliated." Her fear increased. "My brain would freeze up, and I wouldn't be able to respond. I'm not smart enough . . . I'd get rejected and lose my income."

Leila figured she would be stumped by questions about various foods. Clearly, her expectations of herself were both irrational and excessively high; no cook knows everything about every kind of food, how to prepare it, and its nutritional value!

This was time for a cognitive interweave so that she could access information stored in another part of her brain. I said, "You need to adequately prepare as you did with the exam. You won't know all of the answers, but you will know enough to pass." She agreed and did another set of eye movements as she thought about that.

She felt excited as she thought of learning more about foods: their benefits and how different foods affect the body. "I was successful in school in New York. (She had done well in a food and restaurant school when she first came to the U.S. eleven years ago.) I know my mind can open up and absorb the information I need. I did it before."

The interweave had worked. Leila had remembered her prior successes and could feel the sensations as well as recall the images. As she continued moving her eyes back and forth, she remembered her skills and abilities in that venue and realized, *"I don't have to know everything—I can learn."* She concentrated on that for another set.

Then, Leila had a major realization. Because her family had

been uneducated, they were not *able* to answer questions Leila asked when she was a child. Instead, they would put her down. "It was a defense my family used so *they* would not feel stupid. They didn't feel smart enough so they made me feel bad. I stopped asking questions because of their response—they didn't know the answers. They transferred their fears and their own feelings of inadequacy to me." More new positive self beliefs replaced the old negative ones. *"I got a lot of rotten lessons, and I need to take it gently with myself. I am good enough, and I know enough about food. I love reading food books. I'm not afraid of it. I can excel."*

She envisioned doing what she needed to do to get the job she wanted. After she finished the set, she said enthusiastically, "It feels good! It's exciting! I'm excited about doing it. I need to put the excitement into it at each moment."

Leila beamed when she next entered my office and excitedly told me all that had changed in her life. Our last EMDR® processing session had been a huge breakthrough.

Since then, she had received two job offers: one entailed cooking for an adolescent treatment center and the other was cooking for a traveling rock and roll group. If she took the former, she could also cater special events—something she would love to do. A world of possibilities was opening for her. No longer was she worried that no one would want to hire her; rather, now she worried about which job would be the best one for her! Leila exuded self-confidence and felt great!

She no longer worried about not knowing everything. Although that concern had surfaced twice since our last session, she was unfazed. Also, the problem of not feeling smart enough had vanished. Leila had been at a gathering with "very intelligent people" who had formerly intimidated her, but she didn't feel the least bit inferior.

I saw her three more times, and her joy, self-confidence, and self-esteem increased steadily. She felt that a world of opportunities was open to her and that "things were all falling into place." Despite many changes and losses, she felt good about herself and was moving on with her life.

When I spoke with her a year later, she was feeling terrific. She said that the EMDR® work had empowered her. From her hopeless "Oh, my God! What am I going to do?" stance she had moved to "Look at all of the options I have!" She had retained her positive self-beliefs and said, *"I am good enough. I can ask for what I want. I believe in myself. I can take care of myself."* At the time of our last conversation, Leila was still cooking for the adolescent treatment center and enjoying her work. She said, "I am totally self-sufficient, and it feels great! Not depending on a man is freeing." It was a joy to speak with her.

MARLA'S STORY: FROM SELF-HATE TO SELF-LOVE

Marla almost committed suicide one weekend after being laid off from a job she loved. Fortunately, Marla drove to the local crisis center instead. Several days later, a lovely large-sized woman entered my office, having been referred to me by her long-time therapist in the town where Marla had lived for thirteen years before her recent move to northern California.

Excerpts from her journal reflect her state of mind when she first came to see me. "My early childhood, in the words of Erica Jong, was 'a place of refuge and a place of fear.'" By age ten or eleven, tormented by classmates and so-called friends, Marla had created a third place: a place of hope.

Herein, she determined to "show them." She would become a great and famous person, impervious to their taunts, and her tormentors "would feel ashamed and see themselves as the little creatures they were." However, by age forty-three, Marla's place of hope had burned out. Fear had overtaken her and she sought refuge in suicide.

She prepared for this ultimate act of control in her life. She taped the music that she wanted played at her memorial, wrote a will, and executed a Living Will and Physician Directive stating that she did not want extraordinary means enacted to keep her alive; and, she placed these items on her dining room table. In the study, she wrote a suicide note on the computer. Killing herself was the only task awaiting completion.

However, Marla found one last place of refuge. She called the suicide prevention hotline. She was crying, but she was still in control.

"The woman on the other end of the line gave me a standard pep talk that was not going to convince me to stop my plans. I could see through her phone pitch. She even said that many people would be devastated and that she would be too. She didn't even know me. Why should she care? If she really knew me, she'd probably figure like everyone else that I did something wrong and deserved the sinking course of my life. She gave me the name of the closest crisis center after asking if anyone was at home to be with me. Michael, my lover, was at work. I had called him and asked when he was coming home because I had lost my job and I needed him. He said he'd be home soon. To me, that wasn't soon enough.

"But something kept me on the phone with this nameless woman long enough to promise that I'd call her once I got to the crisis center. I left a quick note for Michael and drove, mixed up, confused, and aware of driving while I was crying and not wanting to hurt anyone else as I drove the five miles to the hospital."

Guilt and self-hate festered. Even though Marla told herself that she "could handle the world and its shit," the words and axioms that had been in her mind for forty-three years were stronger than her self-love: "If you follow the rules and do what you're supposed to do, you'll have everything you ever wanted," "If you'd just lose weight, people would like you more," "If you wear this, you'll look pretty, and then I'll want to be seen in public with you," "If you had helped your mother more, she wouldn't be in the hospital and your dad wouldn't have lost your house," "If you hadn't been in the hospital when you were nine years old, we wouldn't have lost our house due to the doctor bills," "If you hadn't done something wrong, you'd still have your job because no boss is going to get rid of a valuable worker," "If you agree with me, I'll love you," "If you are like your older sister, we'll love you," "If you weren't getting hurt all the time and stopped being a hypochondriac, people would like you better," "Stop crying!" "Stop panicking!" "It doesn't hurt."

Marla felt as if no one understood her. "They didn't get it. Life *did* hurt. My childhood hurt. My fantasies hurt because they could never come true. For so long my place of hope was my determination to be a great person. Now I didn't even have that. I couldn't make my life what I needed it to be . . . except over."

In desperation, Marla telephoned her former therapist from the pay phone in the hall of the crisis center. "Bob had helped me many times in the past without ever judging me or my actions. That nonjudgmental concern had helped me through many rough times." He urged her to pursue EMDR® and gave her names of several therapists.

We spent our initial time together reviewing Marla's life. With a sister sixteen months older than she and a brother three years younger, she was the "accident"—the child who shouldn't have been born. She never felt wanted by her parents. "I was told by my mom that she was using two different kinds of birth control when she got pregnant with me." That "lesson" was held up to Marla many times to teach her that she was to "stay a virgin until I was married—because 'birth control doesn't work in our family.' Babies come whether they're wanted or not. I got the picture about my worth at birth."

Marla, overweight in childhood, was compared mercilessly to her slim, blond, older sister who was favored by her parents. Her parents dressed the girls in identical styles but different colors, even dressing her younger brother for Christmas card photographs in shorts of the same fabric. "Everything was supposed to turn out all right. But I was not all right. They knew it, and I knew it. It was obvious, I was a fat kid."

She did not feel understood, supported, or listened to by her parents. Furthermore, they did not value her academic achievement. When Marla was accepted to enter one of the nation's most prestigious nursing schools, her parents refused to pay her tuition—despite their paying for her sister's community college tuition. "Instead of books for college, one Christmas I received a bowling ball—so that our family could go bowling together. What I wanted was not what my parents wanted. All they wanted was for me to look good and be more like my sister."

As an adult, Marla became a talented writer and educator. However, for various reasons, many of her jobs didn't work out as she had desired. Her disappointment fed her feelings of low self-worth and hopelessness.

She chose to begin her first EMDR® processing session by investigating why she had not been able to stand up to her boss who unfairly laid her off from work. She traced her hesitancy to the belief that she was "a bad girl" and associated that belief with the memory of seeing a photograph of herself at age three or four. However, Marla didn't feel strongly about that memory and so dismissed it.

Nevertheless, I urged her to describe the photograph, which "seemed like just a speck" in Marla's memory. She had been hospitalized at the time for a brain concussion she'd incurred when she'd fallen off the kitchen counter onto which she'd climbed.

"I remembered waking up in a hospital, white, black, and gray, no other colors. I was in a crib, and I was too old to be in a crib at home. I saw nurses in white nun's habits across the ward, but no one was with me. I didn't know where I was, but I knew that I must have been really bad to have ended up where I was. I was scared. I felt like I was in a prison for babies because of the bars on the crib."

I adjusted the light bar to a speed comfortable for Marla, and as her eyes followed the green dots of light, feelings that had been hidden for forty years burst forth.

"I'm not a baby! Why am I in a crib? I'm scared! Where are Mommy and Daddy? They're not here because I was bad. I climbed on the counter and fell off. That's why I'm in this crib—it's jail! I'm sorry, Mommy. I'm sorry, Daddy. Please let me out of here. I'll be good, I promise. I promise. Please, please love me again."

Marla relived waking up in that antiseptic hospital without warmth or love or anyone to comfort her. As an adult, with EMDR® she could verbalize what she was unable to say when she was a three-year-old.

With more eye movements, she linked this early memory to other hospital stays. At three years old she had a tonsillectomy; now, she smelled and tasted the ether. She was nauseous and afraid. Next, she was jealous of the attention her sister received. Marla felt unloved again.

Another hospital memory came to mind. This time she was seven or eight years old and was hospitalized for two weeks due to rectal polyps. This was a very humiliating experience. Groups of medical interns examined her rectum and made embarrassing comments without regard for her feelings. The shots were painful too.

"I wasn't supposed to have any feelings or needs." Again, she felt abandoned and unloved.

With the next set of eye movements, she remembered her father bringing a TV into her hospital room and felt his love and concern. Then she remembered her father joyfully spraying water on their backyard lawn—in the middle of a freezing Minnesota winter—to create a private family skating rink! She recalled feeling deeply happy as she and her siblings skated to the music her father played from the phonograph. She smiled. "He took a lot of pleasure in us kids."

We returned to the image of her being in the hospital as a young child, and she now felt "physically bigger." Her anxiety was gone. Her "inner parent" spontaneously began to comfort the child. As an adult, Marla knew what the child in the crib needed and how she had felt. Now, Marla could help that child. Marla's tears of pain became tears of comfort and joy as the child saw a loving face looking down at her. The child felt the loving touch of someone who could pick her up and hold her. And, she also heard the words of a loving parent.

"Oh, honey, I'm so sorry you got hurt. I love you. You are a special and sweet little girl. This shouldn't happen to you. I love you. You must be scared. But I'm here, and I'll take care of you and love you whether you fall off the counter or not. I wish this hadn't happened to you. I'm here. You don't have to feel alone or scared. Would you like a stuffed animal to stay in your bed with you? They put you in a crib so you wouldn't fall out and get hurt more. It doesn't mean that you're a baby. I love you. I'm going to take care of you and protect you. I don't want you to get hurt. I love you." Marla realized she had not been hurt because she was intrinsically bad.

By the session's end, the memory no longer evoked feelings of abandonment or of being bad. Instead, Marla had reprocessed it to a time of feeling loved, a time of warmth. Later, she told me that "dredging up that old memory changed my feelings about that situation so that I felt loved and wanted. That was also the way I'm sure my parents would have wanted it to be for me. I no longer felt abandoned by my parents and exiled into the crib jail. I didn't blame my parents for not being there when I needed them. I had *me* there, for me. My parents couldn't have done for me what I was able to do for myself in the processing. *They* didn't know what I needed, *but I did.* They did what they could back then. My self-parenting supplied the love and comfort and understanding I needed." Marla had tapped into an inner resource that had always been there but from which she had never been able to draw sustenance. I was moved by the beauty and tenderness of Marla's expression of compassion and love for herself.

After leaving this session, Marla "felt drained, but quiet. It was like someone had read my diary and did exactly what I needed to make me feel better. I didn't have animosity for anyone. I had love for that little girl who woke up in the crib jail. And she knew she was loved. That's the reprocessing. No guilt, no blame, just love and caring, which has become a part of me now. One session of EMDR® has not turned my life rosy. But I am still alive in a place of refuge and a place of hope."

The next week Marla no longer felt any pain around that memory. She was less anxious, more self-confident at her new job, and her suicidal thoughts and feelings had stopped. She no longer wanted to hurt herself.

A few weeks later we focused on Marla's belief that "my feelings don't count—I'm not important." She recalled a time when the family was visiting relatives who lived on a farm. "My sister was invited to stay for a week. I wanted to stay too. I was told that I couldn't because I wasn't old enough. I remembered crying and being torn trying to explain to my parents why I should be allowed to stay on the farm. All I was told was that I should stop crying. I said that if I didn't stay on the farm then, I would never get to stay on the farm. Adults told me that I was wrong, but I knew I wasn't, and I never did get to go to the farm. I couldn't stop crying. I was devastated.

No one seemed to care. No one listened. They just wanted me quiet."

We began the EMDR® processing with the image of her crying in the car and hearing her parents saying, "Don't cry! We don't want to hear it anymore." She felt unheard and disconnected from everyone." Soon, she said, "I want someone to say they hear me—to say, 'I'm sorry you're hurting.' A gesture to say 'I'm here.' "

Next she remembered having a broken arm for two weeks before her parents listened to her complaint. She felt unwanted. Medical bills for her frequent injuries and illnesses strapped her financially bound parents.

More memories emerged of her parents giving her the message, "Don't feel and don't tell us how you feel." Then she recalled hurt feelings when boys she liked preferred her sister. A realization popped into her mind. "It's scary to have deep feelings. Whether I feel happy or sad, it seems like no one cares. I have no way of telling people how much I hurt—they don't listen. I'm only a good little girl if I'm not bringing attention to myself and if I don't have any feelings because they don't want to hear them."

Did Marla's parents want to hear about *anyone's* feelings? Marla thought not. She remembered that her father was not listened to either and described her grandmother as "a don't-feel person."

However, she recalled her grandfather's unconditional love. "Grandpa loved me just for me," she said warmly. Happy memories of sitting on her grandpa's lap came to her mind. "Grandpa listened." Despite these happy reminiscences, she identified with not being listened to. She became more and more depressed and helpless. "No sense sticking around if I hurt," she said. "Nobody's going to listen." Emptiness took over.

I saw that her processing was cycling. An interweave was needed to move Marla out of the loop and toward resolution. I asked her to embrace the little girl and listen to her. "Ask her what is in her heart."

"Marla honey, I know you want to stay here on the farm really badly. Let's see what we can do because I love you, and I don't want you to hurt. Let's work something out. This is a hurt we can do something about. So take my hand and let's go see."

That dialogue assuaged Marla's pain. Later, she informed me, "The outcome didn't matter as much as my need for someone to listen to me and acknowledge my feelings. Until that EMDR® session, I never felt listened to. Finally, that memory was defused. I had taken care of myself and found someone, *me*, who listened to that little girl."

Opportunities for Marla to speak out abounded during the next week, and when I saw her next she happily described feeling much more self-confident in all areas of her life. She had filed a formal grievance against her boss, and Marla had personally stood her ground and argued against the unjust charges when challenged by her boss. Furthermore, Marla was happy with the outcome of that encounter. Her suicidal thoughts and feelings were gone and she felt increasingly balanced and strong.

We continued to target Marla's low self-esteem and focused on her belief that "I don't make the right choices," a belief presently stimulated by her mother's disapproval and criticism of Marla's lover and Marla's sense of rejection because she didn't adhere to her mother's ideals. By the end of the session, Marla had replaced that belief with another one: "My mom not liking Michael is no big deal; mothers are like that. I made a good choice with Michael. It is *her* problem if she doesn't approve of him."

Several weeks later, Marla chose to address her irrational fear that Michael would leave her. She related this fear to her traumatic experience of a former lover leaving their ten-year relationship to marry another woman. Continuing to explore, Marla retraced her path to her teenage years.

That was the first time she had considered suicide. "Every time I liked a boy and he would come to my house, he would immediately be attracted to my older and well-endowed blonde sister, Kelly. Once, while playing Ping-Pong with a boy I liked, he and my sister became an item. I went upstairs in tears because boys always liked my sister better than me. I took out a comb and tried to cut my wrists with it. That didn't work so I finally called my mother. My mother tried to comfort me, but she said that if I would lose weight I would be more attractive and then boys would like me. I got the strong message that I wasn't good enough as I was. I was only good enough to be liked if I was skinny and more like my sister."

As she reprocessed this disturbing memory Marla cried that she wasn't a "whole person." She despaired, "Something's missing, and I can't find it. The feeling is the suicidal stuff. My best isn't good enough to keep a job. How can I expect to keep Michael? He will reject me like everyone else has."

Her inner parent stepped in with tremendous compassion. "Honey, you are okay. I love you whether you're dirty, old, happy, or sad. It doesn't matter what you own or have. You are wonderful. I'm so glad you're here. We don't want someone perfect. Here's someone like Michael who accepts the weight and yet encourages fitness and doesn't need to see you smile all the time. He loves you, and I love you. I want you to live without having to conform to other people's expectations."

Marla felt warm and tingly and said the emptiness was getting covered. The scab was gone, and the pain was gone; only tenderness remained.

When we checked with the original picture of being rejected by the teenage boy, the image had changed into her singing joyfully by herself at the top of her lungs in her bedroom. "Who needs them? I can have a lot better time by myself. I need to get closer to me. I am lovable. *I am fine from the inside.* I don't want to think of myself in pictures anymore."

Exhausted, Marla ended the session. She was excited to know herself from her new perspective—from the inside rather than judging herself as she thought others saw her.

At a later time, we had another significant EMDR® processing session wherein we focused on her fear of singing in public. She loved to sing by herself but was terrified of singing in public. Consequently, despite her desire, she was anxious about auditioning for an upcoming musical theater production.

Her fear of singing in public stemmed from humiliation she had suffered in grade school. "In fifth and sixth grades I had the worst time of my whole school life. I was taunted by my classmates, had fat nicknames written across any artwork that I would do in school, and whenever I tried to talk with an adult about how much this hurt me, I was told that if I'd lose weight they'd stop teasing me and I should just ignore the rudeness.

"The worst times were twice a year when the school nurse brought the scale into the classroom for each child's weight and height. The nurse would call out the measurements to the teacher, who usually sat across the room. Naturally, my weight was what everyone was listening for, and then it caused a roar of laughter both in class and on the playground at recess once other kids were told how much I weighed. My parents told me to lose weight if I didn't like it. But, the last time before the measurements were taken, I begged my mother not to make me go back to school, so she wrote a note to the school nurse telling her not to call out my weight. The nurse didn't call out my weight, but she still said it loudly enough for the kids to hear." Marla's psyche interpreted this humiliation as, "If I am myself, people won't like me. Just Marla isn't enough. If I'd lose weight, people would like me." Marla focused on the fifth-grade weigh-in image and became angry that she had been subjected to public ridicule. "I wouldn't let that happen. How dare they allow that to happen?"

She continued, but her tone shifted. "Now I'm sticking up for myself." She imagined her adult self telling the school nurse that the little girl was *not* to be weighed in the class-room. Then, Marla had an epiphany. In an awe-inspired voice, she said, *"When things happen it isn't because I am one way or another; things just happen. Sometimes things work out and sometimes they don't. I may sing well or off-key. It isn't the end of the world one way or another. It doesn't mean anything about who I am."* With that thought she did another set of eye movements.

We returned to the original classroom scene. "I can hear the kids taunting and saying things and it doesn't have the same trigger," she told me. "I'm not going to do things I don't want to do. I feel I'm in a position of strength rather than weakness." Tears streamed down Marla's cheeks as she realized, "I'm with me. I have the strength and compassion to take care of myself; losing weight and having money and boyfriends are not the things I need."

She smiled and said that she felt "really good." Indeed, this self-love was good food for Marla! "I feel intrinsically powerful. I don't need other people's approval. *I like me. I love myself from the parenting point of view. I really like me. I haven't felt this before—from the inside, not judging from the outside.*"

She returned to the original picture of being weighed. "I'm not there," she said. "I'm not being weighed. It did happen, and it hurt, and it won't happen again. I might have had forty years of pain, but I have forty years that can be better."

She imagined singing at the audition the next day and now understood that how she performed had no bearing whatsoever on her self-worth. "This is me. If you don't like it, here is the door, and you are shortsighted. If I get up and sing, I'm going to have a good time. Whether I'm chosen or not has no connection at all with my self-worth. It's okay to sing off-key. It's okay to not be liked by people." In her imagination she was no longer anxious and she exclaimed, "I'm going to have fun!"

In fact, the audition went better than she had ever imagined possible. She was asked to sing unaccompanied and sang her heart out and had a great time on stage. And, she got the part! She happily recounted her experience to me the next week, and her new life-affirming beliefs seemed well-entrenched. "I love my life," she said joyfully. "I feel in charge of my life. I feel like I'm in control. I have choices."

We worked together for a few more months, but the bulk

of the clearing had been completed in the aforementioned EMDR® processing sessions. Marla's deep sense of self-acceptance and self-love continued, and she was very happy in her relationship with Michael. Her fear that he would abandon her never returned.

Marla is confident that she can handle what life brings her. She sang in the musical theater production for several months, found meaningful work, and despite the difficulties she encounters at her job and recurrent job insecurity, she continues to experience inner balance and peace.

CHAPTER 9

Discovering the Transpersonal

I have been using EMDR® for nearly four years now, and the only problem I have is containing my profound awe and continuing appreciation for this remarkable procedure. Leading a client through an EMDR® session is a deeply moving experience for me. It is something like being a midwife for the birth of the Self. Some clients labor long and hard, while others breeze right through—but all experience some level of bliss when their true Self emerges free of the negative influences of their past— in all its beauty, purity, and grace.
          —Bea Scarlata, M.A., L.P.C. EMDR® therapist

It is difficult to describe to people who have not had direct experience with EMDR® either as a client or as a therapist the feeling of awe and grace that one feels with the completion of an EMDR® processing session. There is a sacred feeling in the room. A Canadian psychiatrist described it as a kind of euphoria that is shared between the client and therapist which creates a deep bond. I ran into a colleague of mine at a recent EMDR® Level II training whom I hadn't seen in a long time. She had been using EMDR® in her practice for only a few weeks but felt deeply inspired by the transformations she was witnessing in her clients. "This is spiritual," she said. "I believe it somehow opens the heart to a deep wellspring of healing love." One of my psychology doctoral students called me out of the blue a few months after taking my EMDR® course. He had been very skeptical about EMDR® during the class—as were many of the students. He was now enthusiastic about EMDR® after having used it in his internship setting with a number of clients, many of whom had been terribly abused in the past. Three of the four clients with whom he had worked had what he described as spiritual experiences, and the terrible abuse they had suffered had been transformed.

As a result of EMDR® processing, clients often spontaneously have transpersonal or "beyond the ego" experiences. These experiences of something beyond the personal self take many different forms and may include other states of consciousness such as transcendence and ecstasy, psychic experiences that transcend space and time, spiritual experiences of enlightenment, deep self-awareness, mysticism, epiphanies, spiritual insights, profound experiences of love and compassion for self and others, forgiveness, dramatic energy releases, experiences of bliss and sensory enhancement, experiences of peace and equanimity, and a deep sense of well-being.

When a client has a transpersonal experience, there is always a sense of awe in the room that I share with him or her. We are often moved to tears by the beauty of what has transpired. These experiences have come to clients who have not had any prior religious or spiritual interest or inclination as well as to those who have in the past been spiritually oriented.

Although clients' stories throughout this book have included transpersonal experiences, I want to highlight particular kinds of experiences that occur frequently to EMDR®

clients. These experiences include objective forgiveness, profound experiences of love, trust in life, openings to creativity, heightened sense of well-being, experiences of spiritual liberation and freedom, and spiritual insights and epiphanies.

Objective Forgiveness

During EMDR® processing sessions, clients often experience a spontaneous feeling of forgiveness toward themselves or someone who had harmed them in the past. Dr. Sandra Wilson, in her study of EMDR®'s effectiveness with traumatized clients, found in her fifteen-month follow-up study that many of the participants experienced forgiveness toward the ones who had harmed them. This is not a sentimental forgiveness, based on an idea of what one should feel, nor is it forced or prescribed by the therapist. Rather, this objective forgiveness emerges organically when clients trust themselves to fully feel and process their feelings of anger, sadness, and betrayal. Clients naturally come to see events from the past objectively without the former emotional charge. From this "global perspective" one "sees" all of the parts of a situation, including one's own part, as if from above the scene. One feels a part of a greater impersonal whole. One perceives a "greater order."

Objective forgiveness often arises when clients understand that forgiving is not forgetting. They can then let go of the past as it is held in their bodies and minds. When they see that it does *them* no good to hold onto the angry feelings, the feelings clear and leave the clients at peace. I want to note that forgiveness *may or may not* arise on the part of someone who has been harmed by another; its absence is *not* an indication that something is wrong with the client or that he or she needs to do something. This feeling of forgiveness arises spontaneously like grace and blesses the one who experiences it. Jan was a client who received such a blessing during an EMDR® processing session.

JAN'S STORY

Jan was a psychology graduate student who sought EMDR® therapy because she suffered acute test anxiety of paralytic proportions. She could not make herself study and was terrified that she would fail her course. After the first history-taking session, she felt ready to begin the EMDR® processing.

She began the session by focusing on an image of sitting at her desk with the test in front of her. She felt tremendous panic and anxiety. Her stomach was in a tight knot. Her belief that accompanied the image was, "I have to be perfect."

Soon after beginning the eye movements she began to shake uncontrollably and to sob. Apparently, Jan had recalled a terribly disturbing abuse memory from early childhood. Finally, after several minutes of intense emotional release, she appeared calm.

At the time, Jan was about six years old and was just learning to read. She sat in the living room and was attempting to read a Dr. Seuss book to her mother. Jan stumbled over the words, and her mother became impatient. As little Jan became more anxious, her reading became more disjointed and infuriated her mother. With wild, bloodshot, crazy-looking eyes, she grabbed Jan, tied her to the bed, and beat her mercilessly with an extension cord. Welts appeared all over Jan's little body.

Jan saw the connection between her belief that she had to perform perfectly on her present-day test and the belief that she had developed as a child that she had to perform perfectly for her mother or she would be hurt. Next, Jan processed tremendous rage toward her mother. How could she have treated Jan that way? Ah ha! Jan suddenly knew the answer: because her mother had a mental illness. Her mother *was* crazy.

Jan became furious with her father who had left her as a young child with her crazy mother. "He must not have loved me if he could leave me with her," she whispered. All her life Jan had felt unlovable because of her perceived abandonment by her father and the terrible abuse inflicted on her by her mother. Deep sobs racked Jan as she processed her feelings of being unloved.

Suddenly, Jan realized that she *was* loved by her father. In fact, he had left her mother when Jan was fifteen months old for reasons that had nothing to do with Jan. Jan saw that her belief that she was not lovable had nothing to do with her father's departure; in this moment, she could view the situation objectively. Suddenly, she saw everything in perspective. This insight changed her life.

"My mother's whipping me had nothing to do with me—it was something that happened—it is not who I am." Here, Jan stated an obvious truth. Prior to this session she had unconsciously believed that her mother's abuse *did* relate to Jan's self-worth. If her mother beat her, Jan must have been bad and deserved it. This erroneous belief had persecuted Jan all of her life and affected her self-esteem and relationships.

With Jan's next set of eye movements, a desire to forgive her mother for the abuse emerged spontaneously. "If I forgive, I'll be vulnerable" occurred to Jan immediately. A series of insights associated with forgiveness unrolled: "When I was a child I believed that if I forgave her and let go of my anger, I would be vulnerable and could be hurt. I believed I had to stay strong to survive. I believed my anger made me strong.

But I am an adult now and can take care of myself. If I don't forgive and let go of the past, I'm hurting myself. *I'm* the one who is carrying this pain inside. Forgiving is not forgetting. I will never forget what happened, but I can let go of the pain and anger. I can forgive *now* without compromising myself."

Jan moved her eyes back and forth and imagined forgiving her parents. She felt profound love for herself and for them. Spontaneously, she saw herself blessing her mother. With tears streaming down Jan's cheeks, she thanked her professor whose test she had dreaded for giving her the opportunity to learn the lessons she had just learned. She had gained a global perspective of the events that had transpired in her life and felt compassion for all who had been involved.

Finally, without any direction from me, Jan imagined taking the test and ran through the whole scene in her mind. Afterward, she said that she had felt confident; she had not felt even a trace of anxiety. She no longer believed that she had to be perfect. She believed she was fine as she was; her performance would no longer define her.

When Jan left the session, she felt vibrant and alive—more alive than ever before. Her heart was full of love for herself and her parents and she felt at peace. A feeling of having been touched by grace filled the office. It was a truly awesome experience.

PROFOUND EXPERIENCES OF LOVE FOR SELF AND OTHERS

I have found in my work over the years that most people have difficulty loving themselves. Many people have a severe "inner critic," an inner voice that constantly tells them that they are

not good enough. This feeling of not being good enough often
resides in the area of the heart and is experienced as a con-
striction or chronic heaviness. For many people, this difficulty
in loving themselves also extends to others. They feel re-
strained in the open expression of love, and this blockage is
terribly painful.

I have been moved countless times during EMDR® processing sessions as clients who have never had an inkling of
self-love have experienced their hearts opening to themselves.
Access to this vast reservoir of love was blocked by early conditioning; as the conditioning is cleared by EMDR® processing, clients tap into this natural, abiding resource. Often this
occurs when clients witness their child selves from an adult
perspective. When the adult witnesses the child being hurt,
humiliated, criticized, or misunderstood, the client realizes the
child's fundamental innocence. "I am not bad because I made
a mistake" is an obvious truth. Frequently, clients gain a
transpersonal perspective—one that views life events from a
global perspective. Understanding transcends the narrow egoic
perspective, and compassion often spontaneously arises for
the child self. As the adult self, while doing eye movements,
holds and comforts the child self, feelings of self-love and
compassion flood the entire system—body, mind, and emotions. Clients feel profoundly cleansed by this love. They describe the feeling as holy.

This book has many examples of this self-love arising spontaneously during or after EMDR® processing. The self-love is
a natural byproduct of the clearing of self-hate seeded by
childhood experiences. For my clients, these experiences of
self-love have become a wellspring from which they draw
throughout their lives. After a particularly profound experi-

ence of love for herself and others, one woman said, "This is who I am, this love."

GARY'S STORY

Gary was concerned about his twelve-year-old son, Todd. Todd was a quiet boy, who didn't have a lot of friends. He didn't fit in with the other kids. As Gary voiced his concern, he began to cry. Todd had always been an introverted child, Gary told me, preferring his own company to that of boisterous and rambunctious kindergarten classmates. Gary remembered worrying about Todd then and meeting frequently with Todd's teacher.

Gary thought that something was terribly wrong with Todd and pushed him to socialize more. I sensed that anger underlay Gary's concern and Gary admitted to feeling frustrated and estranged. Clearly, Gary's worry about Todd was out of proportion to the situation. But, what was this all about?

Because Gary had difficulty retrieving a belief or memory about himself that seemed related to this problem, we began with an image of Todd playing alone in the kindergarten class. Gary believed, "There is something wrong with him." As Gary said this, he began to weep. Gently tapping on his knees, I instructed him to "go with that."

Gary was overwhelmed and continued to weep. When he finally stopped crying, he said, "The image right away changed to me as a kid. I was always shy and didn't have a lot of friends. I liked playing by myself. I got an image of my mother's face. She was angry with me. She was telling me there was something wrong with me because I didn't want to go out and play with other kids. She was really upset. I didn't want to hurt my mother. I felt like I was really bad." Gary began to cry again, doubling over in his chair as he sobbed. "Let it pass through," I said softly as I tapped on his knees.

"I really felt like there was something terribly wrong with me," Gary continued. "My mother was so anxious and worried about me. I felt like I was hurting her. I feel so bad about myself."

In the next round of processing, Gary had an insight. "I was just a shy kid. There was nothing wrong with me."

Then Gary imagined holding his child self and comforting him. "You're fine just the way you are. I love you just as you are. It's okay to be shy," Gary sobbed. This time his tears were not because of sadness; they were the cleansing tears of profound self-love. As he cried, he rocked back and forth, exuding love and compassion for the little boy who had been so misunderstood.

Gary realized, "I've done to Todd what my mother did to me," and again began to weep. I tapped on his knees, and after a few minutes his grief subsided. He looked up at me and said, "Todd is fine the way he is and I love him dearly." Gary's heart opened to his son, and Gary again wept tears of profound love and compassion—this time for Todd. Gary imagined holding Todd and telling him what was in his heart.

Gary was exhausted—and deeply moved—at the end of the session. For the first time, he had experienced fully loving himself and his son. This love had always been present but had been blocked by Gary's childhood conditioning. With this cleared, he was filled with the love that was his natural birthright.

TRUST IN LIFE

For the mind in Harmony with the Tao,
all selfishness disappears.
With not even a trace of self-doubt,
you can trust the universe completely.
All at once you are free,
with nothing left to hold on to.
All is empty, brilliant,
perfect in its own being.
                —Seng-ts'an, "The Mind of Absolute Trust"

As I described in Chapter 3, EMDR® helps many clients develop greater trust in life and an increased ability to fully experience life. Some clients sense the presence of a power much greater than they during the EMDR® processing, and their experience engenders comfort and ease.

SUSAN'S STORY

Susan, a client I'd worked with in the past and described in Chapter 8, came to me for an EMDR® processing session a few days prior to her scheduled surgery for the removal of ovarian cysts. She wanted to clear any old memories from her body and mind associated with a traumatic surgery twenty years before that she felt might interfere with her state of mind and subsequent healing from the current surgery. Although her doctor didn't foresee any problems with the surgery, she faced a number of unknowns. The cysts could be malignant, scarring from the past surgery might necessitate more extensive work than anticipated, and the surgeon might have to remove Susan's ovaries.

As a self-employed, single woman living alone, the possibility of an extended recuperation worried Susan. Many fears and anxieties floated just beneath the surface of her mind. Who would take care of her? How would she survive? How would she feel about losing her ovaries? What if the doctors botched the surgery and harmed her? Could she trust them?

We began the EMDR® processing session by focusing on her worst fear. "They'll open me up and find all kinds of scarring inside of me which will complicate the surgery. Someone'll make a mistake and I'll suffer for it." Susan's stomach was tense and nervous.

She quickly reprocessed the earlier traumatic surgery, which had entailed a long recovery time. She remembered how difficult it had been for her at that time, but she also recalled the support she had received from her friends. She remembered that although she now lived alone, she had many friends who loved her and had offered her their comfort and support before and after the current surgery.

Next, she imagined losing her ovaries. Although she was past menopause, she still felt emotionally attached to them. But, during the processing, she could say good-bye to them; she thanked them for their years of service. Then she felt at peace with the possibility of losing them.

She proceeded to the fear that her surgeon would have a bad day, perhaps due to insufficient sleep the prior night, and would possibly make a mistake. She feared not being in control; literally, her life was in the hands of others.

This thought led to an epiphany! An image of large loving hands came into her mind. She said aloud, *"I feel my life is in hands much larger than my own. My life is in God's hands,"* and felt a deep sense of release and trust. Her need to control things vanished and a sense of ease permeated her body.

Then, as Susan imagined the day of surgery, she felt free of anxiety. "I will be surrounded by the love of my friends as I go into surgery, and I know I will be okay no matter what the outcome. I am in the care of hands much greater than my own. I can trust that and let go."

After the surgery, Susan called to tell me that everything had gone well. She had not been anxious and her "heart was open." She was healing well and thanked me warmly for the work we had done.

INCREASED CREATIVE EXPRESSION AND A HEIGHTENED SENSE OF WELL-BEING

For many clients EMDR® processing clears impediments to their creative expression and sense of well-being. I believe that everyone has different natural gifts and talents that become blocked from expression by early conditioning. As I described earlier, this conditioning is like clouds that obscure the sun. The sun is always there but not always apparent. EMDR® processing helps to clear the conditioning, like the clouds, so that one's inherent creativity can be expressed. Following EMDR® processing sessions, artistically inclined clients have often spontaneously begun to paint, draw, take photographs, compose music, or write poetry.

ANDREW'S STORY

Andrew, a fifty-five-year-old engineer, opened quite dramatically to his creativity in this way. His EMDR® sessions stimulated "transcendent visionary experiences." Andrew sought treatment because he was depressed, highly anxious, and felt that his life "wasn't in order." Although he had been in psychotherapy sporadically for a long time, he had never found the relief he desired from his symptoms. An important piece of Andrew's history was that his father had been a tyrannical and physically abusive man who had made Andrew's childhood miserable.

After about six EMDR® processing sessions, which focused on the childhood abuse and current life difficulties, Andrew experienced tremendous relief from his symptoms. His gloom and feeling of being a failure vanished. His anxiety lessened markedly and he became excited about his business. More remarkable, however, was the spiritual transformation he experienced as a result of the sessions.

Andrew had no prior interest in spirituality or religion; he had rejected organized religion long ago. What he experienced after EMDR® processing sessions was beyond anything he had previously known or heard about. About an hour or two after the processing sessions, he experienced an extraordinary intensification of his sensory system, particularly color and shape perception. Two years prior, Andrew had lost some of his visual sensitivity and was frustrated with his painting and photography. One day after an EMDR® processing session, he had a transcendental experience of enhanced sensory perception that filled him with awe.

"After leaving a bookstore I looked up at a stone tower at the church on the corner. It is a square tower, and the stonework has a lot of relief. There are lights illuminating this tower. I couldn't believe how beautiful the tower was! I could see every highlight and shadow so clearly! It seemed to shine in the night! It was very, very beautiful! No one could portray that tower more beautifully than my vision!" He described this remarkable vision as being unlike anything he had ever experienced before and one that filled him with wonder. It felt like a "miracle."

As a result of these sessions and his enhanced sensory perception, Andrew opened to his creative expression. He had always been extremely visually-oriented and creative, but his early childhood abuse had blocked the expression of his creativity. With the blockages cleared by his EMDR® processing, visual images constantly drew his attention and he began to do more photography and drawing. "It was like my vision was widened and sped up. I found myself looking out more at the world and being taken in by the beauty around me." He also began to design the advertising for his business instead of hiring someone else to do it because now he could express artistically what he wanted to capture. He was excited and enthusiastic.

Along with the freeing of his creative expression, Andrew also experienced a profound opening of his heart and felt love for and connected to all of humanity. "After an EMDR® session I felt like I wanted to go out and hug everyone I saw." He journaled, "I have seen the light! That is the way I feel. I feel better all the time. And, now I understand how we are all connected as humans throughout the world." He had overcome his sense of separateness and alienation.

A year later, Andrew's beautiful sense of well-being has continued as a subtle background of his everyday life. "I just feel better! I have a heightened sense of well-being that I never had before. I am experiencing this over a long period of time, not just in short bursts." Because of EMDR® he feels an omnipresent reservoir of well-being that he can draw on whenever he feels the need. "I have a new confidence that I have this resource inside myself. It is my own source and doesn't come from outside of myself."

I have witnessed other clients' experiencing similar feelings to Andrew's. Craig, for example, had a deep love of music but because of traumas in his life had developed a severe inner critic. The EMDR® processing opened his heart and his creative expression and he spontaneously began to compose songs, which were beautiful expressions of his wholeness. Musical expression brought him tremendous joy. Craig also experienced blissful energy releases in his body and a heightened sense of well-being. Once he felt "ecstatic energy" moving up his spine following the clearing of old material and on many other occasions he experienced joyful releases in the area of his heart. He described his experience as "a sacred sphere of radiance" that spread "blissful energy" throughout his body. As this radiance emanated from his heart, he felt love for all of humanity and a desire to help others.

EXPERIENCES OF SPIRITUAL FREEDOM

The fanciful idea of a self is a contraction, a limitation of wholeness, real being. When this notion dies we find our natural expansion, stillness, globality without periphery or center, outside or inside. Without the notion of an individual there is no sensation of separateness and we feel a oneness with all things.

—Jean Klein, *Who AM I?*

Many EMDR® clients have glimpses of enlightenment or moments of liberation from self-concepts. These glimpses evoke a feeling of freedom in the body and mind. There is a sense of expansion and dissolving of boundaries that may be felt as very blissful. It feels sacred. Peter had such an experience.

PETER'S STORY

Peter came to me because he was feeling stuck in his life. Although he had a degree from a prestigious law school and was multilingual, he worked in a job that he didn't like and that was below his experience and educational level. Self-doubt and self-criticism plagued him and kept him from pursuing the career he most desired. He believed, "I'm not good enough," "I'm not qualified," "I don't deserve a job I love," and "I'd screw it up if I got it."

Much of our EMDR® processing work focused on targeting and processing his self-limiting beliefs, which had developed from living with a physically abusive, alcoholic father. This unfortunate man had never actualized his potential and vented *his* frustration on his family. Peter's father wanted his son to be successful in the world so that Peter's success would reflect positively on him, Peter's father, but he also wanted his son to fail so Peter wouldn't surpass him. This double message kept Peter in a perpetual bind.

During one particularly powerful EMDR® processing session, Peter realized set after set how he had always tried to fulfill his parents' expectations of him. He based his life decisions on what he thought others wanted him to do. He realized, "I look for external validation to prove I'm okay. I look for things outside myself to bolster my self-esteem. I need external validation of my self-worth."

With the next set of eye movements he had what he called an "Ah ha!" experience. He saw that his mother and father had been bound by *their* parents' concepts and expectations and had passed this legacy on to him. This conceptual straitjacket had confined generation after generation, defining who they were and what they could expect from their lives. The unconscious expectations were repeatedly imposed on following generations. Peter grasped this from a dispassionate global perspective. He saw how he had always tried to fit into this conceptual mold, which was a prison with invisible bars. In seeing the prison for what it was, Peter was freed from it momentarily. Liberation was in the seeing. He experienced an upwelling of deep feeling and a release of energy; he felt joy and bliss, and tears streamed down his face.

"Who I am has nothing to do with other people's definition of me. When passion comes from deep inside it has integrity. The only genuine way to live is to let the passion come up in me and guide me. This is freedom. This is what God's will is."

Peter realized that "God's will" was to express his creativity without the constraints of limiting concepts—for they were simply that, just concepts. His global objective seeing freed him from them, and the freedom liberated contracted energy in his body. He felt this energy originating in his heart and flowing throughout his body; he was awed and extremely inspired. Peter left the session affirming, "I can accept and embrace my passion—the will of God—in every way and have the courage to act and trust in that."

Spiritual Insights and Epiphanies

Momi's Story

> For what is it to die but to stand naked in the wind and to
>   melt into the sun?
> And what is it to cease breathing, but to free the breath
>   from its restless tides, that it may rise and expand and
>   seek God unencumbered?
> Only when you drink from the river of silence shall you
>   indeed sing.
> And when you have reached the mountain top, then you
>   shall begin to climb.
> And when the earth shall claim your limbs, then shall you
>   truly dance.
>   —Kahlil Gibran, *The Prophet*

Opening to our greatest fear—dying—can bring freedom, truth, and understanding. I have witnessed many clients whose lives were ruled by this fear become free by fully facing it and imagining their own deaths during EMDR® processing sessions. After surviving their imagined deaths, clients have had transpersonal insights and epiphanies which have expanded their personal view.

Ramana Maharshi, one of the greatest spiritual teachers of the twentieth century, faced his fear of death and experienced spiritual enlightenment. When he was seventeen years old, Ramana became terrified at the thought of his own death. He went into his room that night, lay down, and pretended to die. He was determined to fully face death. Out of this experience came his realization *that the body dies but consciousness is not touched by death.* "I am immortal consciousness." He realized that consciousness is never born and never dies: it *is* always. Maharshi reported later that these realizations "went through me like a powerful living truth that I experienced directly, almost without thinking. 'I' (i.e., the true I or Self) was reality, the only reality in this momentary state. All conscious activity that was related to my body flowed into this 'I'. From that moment, all attention was drawn as if by powerful magic to the 'I' or 'Self.' The fear of death was permanently extinguished. From this time on I remained fully absorbed in the 'Self.' " (*The Spiritual Teaching of Ramana Maharshi*, Shambhala, 1988)

Many of my clients have had spiritual experiences when processing fears or phobias that are rooted in their fear of death. I have found that with EMDR® processing clients can face their fear directly and move through it. In doing so, many clients discover a new relationship to their own mortality that brings them peace and balance. Momi had such an experience.

Momi, a fifty-five-year-old semi-retired mental health professional with an adventurous spirit, lived alone in Hawaii but made frequent visits to the San Francisco Bay area. During her visits we would schedule several sessions and work intensively on her areas of concern.

Her intense fear of flying particularly concerned her, especially since she flew between Hawaii and San Francisco several times a year. Together, we explored her associations to this fear, and she narrowed her fear to the fear of turbulence. The belief she associated with turbulence was, "The plane is going down!" and described a number of frightening times when she'd felt her life was in danger. She'd been particularly terrified by turbulence during an interisland flight in 1991.

Momi recalled her best friend Claudine's death in a plane crash in 1974. Claudine, a young mother of two, and her husband were flying home from a ski trip to Vail, Colorado, when a blinding storm overtook the small craft. The plane crashed into a mountain, and everyone on board was killed. Before embarking on the fatal flight, Claudine had called Momi from the airport and told her that she did not want to go. Momi encouraged Claudine to follow her instincts and *not* go. However, Claudine went anyway.

"When I feel afraid of flying and I'm at the airport, should I listen to the fear and not fly or should I go anyway?" Momi asked me. She realized that she believed that one day she too would die in a plane crash.

Momi stated that she was not at all afraid to die a slow, peaceful death surrounded by friends and family. However, a sudden, violent death frightened her—one for which she would have no preparation or forewarning. She'd be gone in the terrible "bang" of the final impact.

Momi was careful to keep "current" in her relationships. She always settled any disagreements and cleared any problems with friends and family immediately. If she were to die, she felt she would be able to do so without regret. In fact, Momi consciously made her airplane rides an opportunity to be aware of her own mortality. "I notice that when I get on a plane I say, 'Well, is all my business together? Is there any person I haven't said what I needed to say to? Any person I haven't forgiven? And, have I forgiven myself?' I do a little run-through, and usually I'm clean."

Nevertheless, despite Momi's wisdom and awareness, she

was terrified of airplane turbulence. She *dreaded* flying. Adrenaline rushed through her body when there was even the slightest turbulence. Often, she would pester the flight attendants by asking, "Is this a lot of turbulence? Should I be worried?" and carefully observe their behavior to check for any signs of fear they might be concealing.

We began EMDR® with Momi focusing on her most terrifying experience of airplane turbulence. She described the 1991 flight, during which there was a heavy rainstorm with lightning, strong winds, and zero visibility. Momi recalled the image of sitting as the plane lurched up, down, and sideways. Lightning flashed, and she clutched the hand of the small Japanese woman sitting next to her. At this time, Momi told me she felt extremely anxious—ten on the scale of zero to ten. Her stomach was churning, her chest was tight, and adrenaline pumped through her body. "This may be it—the end of my life," she cried in terror. "Oh shit! This is it!"

She followed the green lights of my light bar with her eyes and narrated her mental process. The suddenness of an airplane crash greatly disturbed her. "That's what I *fear* is going to happen, you know. The plane is going down, and I have thirty seconds or a minute to put my life in order or to integrate it all. I think that's what's frightening."

She associated to a fear of being trapped and burning to death as Claudine had, and I suspected there was vicarious traumatization: that Momi had an internal image with accompanying affect that was related to how she imagined her friend had died.

I asked Momi to tell me how Claudine had died, and she answered, "The plane burst into flames on impact, and all their bodies were charred. She was strapped in her seat."

I asked Momi to describe—as if in a movie—how she imagined the moments before and after that crash while Momi continued with the eye movements. I intuited that this imagery underlay her fear of turbulence.

"The plane is going down. The engines are freezing over. There's snow all around us. Totally disoriented. There's so much snow in the air we just don't know where we are— BANG! We hit a mountain! Boom! Consciousness over. The fire comes. I'm not conscious of burning in the fire. It's total— it's utter fear. We don't know where we are and then (Momi clapped once loudly) BANG! I guess that's horrible—that part of not being able to integrate one's life."

Momi began to cry. "Oh, I just feel so horrible and sad for Claudine. How awful! At the prime of her life. What a way to go—being terrified for a few minutes, utterly terrified. And then BANG!"

Momi realized that although she hoped *she* wouldn't die in a plane crash, she *had* grown into the major part of coming into her own. "I'm blooming, and I have been for a number of years. My death wouldn't be tragic like it was with Claudine." This was an insight or realization about herself: she saw the difference between herself at fifty-five years of age and Claudine at age twenty-nine.

Momi returned to the image of Claudine's plane crash and was gripped again with fear. She realized she had to face the terrible BANG! "I need to be able to make peace with that BANG. That's what locks the terror in place. So far I've resisted that. I need to experience BOOM!-It's-all-over." She imagined the moment of impact and her own death as she did the eye movements.

"It's ghastly being literally in a white fog. It's very turbulent, the plane engine is losing control, and the wings are freezing over. You know how you say, 'Oh shit, this is really it,' but you don't really believe it? But you say it, and then BANG! Dead. I mean, unconscious. I think, 'Okay now, it's all over.' Ooooh! BANG! (Clap! She claps her hands to dramatize the bang and pauses.) I'm still alive. (She chuckles and pauses again.) What's nice is I'm still alive; my body's died. But, no fear. There was fear back *there.*"

Momi gained a major insight into her fear of death; she realized that her fear was of *anticipating* death, not of death itself. She imagined being dead and felt no fear.

Spontaneously, she heard Claudine speaking. The "message" was Claudine's description of what her death was like. *"It's only awful fighting it—that was terrifying. The actual BANG was not awful. And after that it was slightly disorienting—as a spirit—but the worst part of the whole thing was those fearful minutes fighting what was so. What was so awful was confusion and unknowingness. We all were terrified, and we were screaming. We all were very afraid and that was hell."*

Claudine's words felt deeply meaningful to Momi, and comforted her. "There's something about what she said. The other side was fine. Even the bang was fine. The actual moment of impact was instantaneous. So she's saying something about when I get in the turbulence and go 'Oooooohhhh,' I'm resisting and fighting it. That's where the hell is, that's where the terror is."

Momi realized she could choose to act differently if her plane was going to crash. "I know that if we do go down, I could enjoy the ride no matter what happens—and, chances are very strong that you're going to make it—over ninety-nine percent!"

Momi again returned to the image of Claudine's death, and as Momi began the eye movements she heard Claudine talking to her again, and what Momi heard changed her view of the meaning of her friend's death.

"Claudine, who's on the other side, is coming over from the other side—sort of turning the clock back and saying, 'Hey, what appears to be frightening doesn't need to be frightening 'cause I've experienced it all the way to the ultimate horrible BANG! which wasn't really so ultimately horrible. You thought it was tragic that I died at the budding of my life. And, from a human-life point of view, it was tragic. But, my time was up. For some of us our time is up when we're two months old. Some of us make it to ninety years old. Some of us make it to one hundred. But, you know, it's only those who are left behind who will judge whether it was tragic or not.' Somehow she's saying that for her it was time."

Momi became aware that she could distinguish the voice of her inner wisdom from the inner voice of fear. She also felt deeply moved: she felt that she has been guided by and protected by a "kind of spiritual guidance."

The next time Momi returned to the image of Claudine's crash, Momi saw two images on a "split screen." One screen showed Claudine's last few minutes before the crash; the other showed the last few minutes on the terrifying interisland flight. Matter-of-factly, Momi told me that "somehow one made it and one didn't, and that's *really* the only truth. The rest is interpretation." Momi knew she might or might not survive a real crash, but chances are that she would. I asked her to "go with that split screen image and the belief that 'I may or may not crash.'"

First, she processed the interisland flight image. Her fear

was manageable; it no longer overrode her. She saw the plane landing safely. Then Momi went to the screen of the fatal crash. She imagined herself in Claudine's situation, one in which Momi *does* crash and die. "We're in heavy duty snow in a small plane, and . . . no, I'll change it. There's thunder and lightning, a big United Airlines plane over the Pacific with no land in sight. That's the usual. The computer fails on the airplane and a wing falls off. It's it, this is it."

She imagined her "spiritual guidance" saying, " 'Momi, this is IT. Prepare to crash.' We may have, if we're lucky, a minute or two or we may have only a second or so, but he is giving me a few seconds. He says, 'That's all you really need—just a few seconds. PREPARE to crash.'

"I picture myself *very* calmly preparing to crash. Totally centered. And that's all it takes. It's not like 'review your life.' He's also saying, 'This can happen: you can have a moment of utter peace—a few seconds before you die—in a horrendous situation. That means keeping your life current and in place all the time. If you don't, you are going to have a horrible death. It is important you keep current with people, the ones you love, the ones you care for. Tell those that you love that you love them. You don't have to tell them, just show them. And those that you're angry or upset with, DEAL with it.'

"I picture—oh, this is wonderful—totally surrendering into this huge impact 'cause there's *nothing* else to do. My whole body . . . everything is exploding in slow motion, and my spirit soars through it—just *goes* with it. I'm very serene."

We were both moved and in awe. Momi had died, and yet her spirit continued. She felt deep peace.

When I asked Momi to look once more at the split-screen and tell me what she saw, she answered, "What comes to mind is: could go, probably won't." She laughed. "Could crash, probably won't." She felt "totally fine."

"It feels really important to say, 'Could go, probably won't,' " she told me. "If I do, I do—I've already at least dealt with it *here*."

She scanned through images with her new belief: "could go, probably won't." The imagery and emotions were completely different! Levity and laughter had replaced the terror. From a transpersonal perspective, Momi no longer felt death to be so serious. I was struck by a sense of rather cosmic glee!

"I picture myself (she is laughing) in the aisle of the airplane now," Momi told me, "sort of ... my spirit is ... I'm still strapped in my seat." "Could go, probably won't. Could go, probably won't," Momi chanted and sang playfully. "I'm going up and down the aisle. I have some rattles in my hand and I go up to someone who's rather scared, and go (she sings), 'We could go, but we probably won't.' Then I've got the whole plane singing 'We *could* go, but we probably won't—cha cha, cha cha cha cha.' We're all having a good time." Momi was elated and laughing merrily as she recounted her imagined flight.

Momi seemed to have cleared her fear so I asked her to imagine her actual flight back to Hawaii the next day. As she imagined that flight, she had a few slightly anxious moments which we quickly cleared with the eye movements. When she imagined turbulence, she felt a little nervous, but she imagined herself doing eye movements to calm herself. That, she explained, helped to "blank the fear mind." Momi felt butterflies, but not terror.

Mostly, she saw herself gleefully singing and dancing down the airplane aisles. "Occasionally, when I see some fear come up, I need this little mantra, 'Could go and probably won't.' It feels fun to sing a song. I don't know if I'll do that or not, but at least in here I'm singing this song and it is very elevating."

Two weeks later Momi told me that the plane ride back to Hawaii had tested our work! About thirty-five minutes into the air, the pilot announced that there was going to be mild disturbance. At that moment, Momi scanned her emotions and found, "I'm fine. Usually I'd be drinking a glass of wine right about now to calm my nerves, especially with any kind of turbulence. Instead I'm noticing that wine *doesn't* appeal to me at all so early in the day. Bottom line: no nerves to calm right now."

Toward the end of the meal service, the pilot ordered the passengers to remain seated with their seatbelts tightened and instructed the flight attendants to take their seats. Thus began the scene of severe turbulence Momi had rehearsed during our session. The plane jolted and made loud creaking sounds. Once again, Momi assessed her state.

"With every jolt, people were yelling in unison, 'Whoa! Whoa! Augh!' I'm not yelling, though my adrenaline is going. I'm laughing! Excited! Afraid. Yet laughing! I take the hand of the guy sitting next to me, who happens to be a flight attendant on vacation, and ask him to give me a running commentary regarding all the turbulence he's ever flown in and how this now compares to other times. He says this is bad, but he has been in worse, though this is longer than usual—about forty-five minutes. I notice I'm wired but not in terror. I sing under my breath, 'Could go, probably won't,' several times, and do some eye movements. The adrenaline rush comes and goes with the jolting movements of the plane, but I'm okay!—not terrorizing myself with images of the plane going down into the sea as I've done many times before."

Momi was excited and aroused as if riding a roller coaster. She didn't need to pray. "I didn't feel traumatized at all by the experience. In fact, if someone had offered me a ticket back to San Francisco, I wouldn't have hesitated to take it."

The rest of the flight went smoothly and was even pleasant. At the baggage area she noticed that some of the passengers were visibly shaken. "One guy was saying, 'Wow! Was that ever rock and roll!' A woman exclaimed, 'Worst flight I've ever been on!' "

As Momi listened to the frightened passengers, she noticed how glad she was about the shift she had made. "Before the EMDR® session I would've been relieved to be alive after such turbulence. This time, though, I'm thinking, wow, the adrenaline was pumping—a real instinctual gut reaction—yet no thoughts of, 'It's all over. Adios, Momi.' " She was free of the old trauma.

"Facing death and going to the other side made a significant impact on my life," Momi told me. She no longer feared flying. Her insights had settled in a deep philosophical way and had permeated her whole life. Whereas she had always thought of Claudine's death as a tragedy, she now saw it from a transpersonal perspective that felt more objective. It had been Claudine's time to die. "It is only from our narrow, human perspective that it seemed wrong." Finally, Momi was at peace with Claudine's death. Momi also felt more ready to accept what life would bring her. "Any day I *could* go, but I probably won't. I feel like I am living more fully in the present."

CHAPTER 10

A Life Transformed:
Melanie's Story

Melanie's story—parts of which I've described throughout this book—weaves together many of the threads that have been presented in the preceding chapters and creates a tapestry that demonstrates the depth and complexity of integrating EMDR® into the context of a longer-term therapy that addresses multiple problems. Hers is an inspiring story of discovery, recovery, and transformation.

Working with Melanie during a three-year period was one of the biggest challenges of my career—and a profound privilege. Feeling at times as if we were descending weekly into hell, we journeyed into the depths of the terrible unknown where unspeakable horrors were revealed to her. Upon her return from the underworld Melanie would seem to have reclaimed another part of her lost self and she felt stronger and more confident about venturing repeatedly into the unknown. Oftentimes, our sessions began with little more than a body sensation, a flashback scene, or a nightmare—we had no idea what would emerge. Because of my faith in EMDR®'s healing power, my ability to be comfortable with not knowing where we were going, and my well-developed intuition, I was able to facilitate her passage through blocked areas.

Melanie came to see me because of her debilitating depression and anxiety. She drank uncontrollably as a way of
coping and had shut down emotionally. She had never been
in therapy and distrusted doctors, but she desperately wanted
to feel better. She wanted her recurrent nightmares to stop,
and she wished to be free of her panic and unmanageable anxiety.

When I first met with Melanie, it was as if she were hiding behind a wall. My challenge was to reach Melanie behind
her wall and form a bond with her. At times, she seemed so
far away.

To her, therapy was a foreign concept. She had few friends
and never revealed her deeper self to anyone. Her relationships—even with herself—were superficial. Melanie, who
was not at all psychologically minded or informed, had never
examined her life. At times in sessions she looked at me with
a look of incomprehension on her face, as though I was speaking a foreign language.

Although Melanie had many symptoms of someone who
had been sexually abused, she had no conscious memory of
such abuse and was shocked when the vivid imagery, body sensations, tastes, and smells emerged that—despite being horrific and difficult to integrate—made sense. She was estranged
from her emotions and felt numb most of the time; she never
allowed any of her feelings to show. She *couldn't* cry. She ignored her body; she skipped meals, ate sugary food for dinner,
never exercised, and drank excessively. She didn't trust other
people and had never been sexually intimate with a man
when she was sober.

Our work entailed three phases. The first phase lasted about
two months during which time we met weekly, developed

rapport, and focused on her becoming sober. We talked during these sessions, and Melanie began a journal. Later, her journal became an invaluable resource for her.

During the treatment's intensive middle phase of processing, which lasted two years, we met twice a week. During a ninety-minute (or longer) EMDR® processing session, we processed emergent abuse memories; later in the week, we met for a fifty-minute integrative session during which we talked about what had come up in the previous EMDR® processing session.

Along with the EMDR®, we used guided imagery. The imagery enabled her to establish a safe place where she went figuratively at the beginning of each session. We also addressed her inner child so that Melanie developed a close compassionate relationship with this aspect of herself, this child self who was so terrified and mistrustful of people and the world. We cleared one horrific memory after another. After each processing session, she immediately felt as if huge weights were removed from her body. Nearly always, she felt calm and peaceful afterward. Eventually, she gained confidence and trusted that we could get through anything together. As her memories surfaced and were processed, her flashbacks, nightmares, and fears decreased—and disappeared.

In conjunction with our work, she consulted with a psychiatrist who prescribed an antidepressant medication for her depression, which, despite the progress in clearing traumas, had not lifted. There was no indication that the medication interfered in any way with Melanie's ability to engage in the EMDR® processing work.

After two years of intensive therapy, Melanie seemed to have reprocessed nearly all of her childhood traumatic events.

Generally, she felt calm and peaceful. Her nightmares had almost entirely ceased, and she reported sleeping well. She felt good about herself and was optimistic about her life and meeting new people. She was attending seminars to further her education, walking in nature, eating well, and exercising regularly.

She felt "neutral" about the abuse perpetrators and felt calm and peaceful—even in the presence of two of them who regularly attended family gatherings. She was able to cry and feel a full range of emotions. She had logged more than two years' sobriety and no longer desired alcohol.

During the third and last phase of therapy, Melanie met with me every other week. In those sessions, we addressed her relationships and deeper questions about life and spirituality. Occasionally, we scheduled an additional EMDR® processing session because a disturbing memory had popped up, but that was rare. Metaphorically, the forest fire had been extinguished, but a spark flared periodically and required attention. The intense work was behind us and there was a peacefulness and nonurgency present in these sessions. Melanie had moved on with her life and was developing the interpersonal skills she'd missed because of the abuse.

For Melanie, writing her account of her experience in EMDR® work with me became part of her healing. "To have my story included in Laurel's book is an enormous opportunity for which I'm very thankful. To be able to break my silence in this fashion will be an extraordinary step toward lifelong healing and peace of mind." Melanie's narrative follows.

MELANIE TELLS HER STORY

THE BEGINNING OF THERAPY

I remember hitting rock bottom—it was Christmas morning and I was horribly hung over—perhaps even still drunk. I was starting to recall that last evening I had once again drunk massive quantities of vodka. This kind of excessive drinking was my routine. During the previous seven months it had become increasingly difficult for me to get that almighty buzz. I just couldn't seem to drink enough, fast enough, to get high.

My purpose in getting drunk was to stop the pain that exploded inside my heart. That I could feel pain was really bizarre since I felt dead—as though trapped in a twilight zone of nothingness. But, somewhere within the murky nothingness was unbelievable pain, and the pain worsened daily. I continued in this horrible emotional state until exhausted by vomiting, diarrhea, headaches, stomach cramps, dizziness, and blackouts.

How did I get to this point? I had always been very successful at keeping my pain out of my direct consciousness. Well, the sudden loss of a job I loved shattered my protective defenses and hurtled me into the darkness of hell, and on Christmas morning I realized—through the alcohol-induced fog of my brain—that I could not continue to live like this. I had two choices: commit suicide or seek help.

Two weeks later I had my first session with Laurel. I don't remember much about that session except that after listening to me for about twenty minutes she said point blank, "You're an alcoholic, and you have to stop drinking in order for me to help you."

I did not believe that I was an alcoholic. I drank too much

sometimes, but it was not a big problem—so I thought. I figured I would just stop drinking for a couple of months, get well in therapy, and then go back to drinking.

When I went to my next session, I was totally freaked out. I was so agitated that I couldn't sit. I paced back and forth until, finally, I plastered myself in a corner and stood there, shaking. I was extremely angry with Laurel—this was her fault!—she's the one who came up with the bright idea and said, "STOP DRINKING!"

Laurel explained that I was going through withdrawal and suggested that I consider checking into a hospital for help through this period. I said, "No way, no hospitals, no doctors—it's just you and me." Being so agitated made me realize, however, that staying sober would not be as easy as I'd thought.

For two months I saw Laurel once a week, and she tried to keep me sober and stabilized. She kept insisting that I was severely depressed and in need of medication, but I wouldn't listen. I thought I was just experiencing alcohol withdrawal and that it would stop soon. But, instead, I kept feeling worse. My twilight zone of nothingness became a swirling black hole, sucking me down.

I stayed sober for two months, struggling all the while against feelings of wanting and needing alcohol and against friends who deliberately tried to sabotage my sobriety. In the end, one of my "good friends" talked me into having "just a couple of drinks because they could not hurt me."

Well, after a couple of drinks at the bar, I went to my usual session with Laurel. As the alcohol wore off, I experienced *a horrible crashing and hitting rock bottom.* I had never felt this before; I felt as if I were on an out-of-control elevator dropping from the fiftieth to the first floor in three seconds. A round of EMDR® revealed that I was getting tired of the constant struggle to keep myself intact and to keep the black hole from devouring me. Also, the processing exposed my suicide plan that I thought was the perfect way to end my pain.

Laurel told me again to stop drinking and to see a doctor for antidepressant medication. This time was different. The past two hours had scared the hell out of me and convinced me that I was pretty sick; I knew I needed to make a total commitment to sobriety.

At this point I began seeing Laurel twice a week, and we worked as a team to keep me sober. I became a very active supporter of my own sobriety; I started reading books and articles regarding alcoholism and how to stay sober. I have not had any alcohol in five years now.

At some point I started attending AA meetings. Initially, Laurel had suggested that I give AA a try, but I resisted because I was afraid of people. However, as I learned how to communicate with and trust Laurel, I developed enough self-confidence to venture a little into the world. At first, the AA meetings were helpful. It was helpful to hear other people's stories and realize that their feelings, problems, and struggles were similar to mine. But I found that with EMDR® I was getting better and moving on with my life while the people in AA were attending endless meetings and talking over and over again about their past problems. I soon realized AA was not for me. I was doing very well in therapy with Laurel; we were uncovering my problems and dealing with them.

THE ABUSE MEMORIES SURFACE—EMDR®
PROCESSING BEGINS

After that pivotal therapy session, I was convinced that I *did* need help for my depression and began medication. Unfortu-

nately, it took three weeks for the antidepressant to work—
and those three weeks felt like eternity. At last, I started to feel
better and thought things would calm down a little for me.

But, no such luck! Nightmares started. In them I was
trapped, couldn't breathe, and felt hot or cold. People were trying to get me. Every morning, I woke up exhausted. I had no
idea where these nightmares were coming from, and I was beginning to suspect that something horrible had happened to
me when I was a little girl.

One day when I was driving home after a session in which
I'd been telling Laurel about my latest nightmare, I felt weird.
Suddenly, fear gripped my entire body. I shook and wanted to
crawl into a corner and cry. I had no idea what had caused this.
My nightmares worsened.

Two days later I called Laurel. I was furious with her. She
had set something off. How could she do that when I was
barely hanging on? She kept telling me that I had to be on stable ground before we could really do any work, but how could
I get there when new crap surfaced all the time?

I was angry, confused, scared, and totally overwhelmed. I
felt as if I were delicate crystal which could shatter into a zil-
lion pieces at any moment.

I wanted to crawl back into a bottle of booze—familiar territory! But my new awareness reminded me that alcohol only
created more pain in my life. It had never helped me. *Thus, I
had no place to go back to. I could only go forward.*

During an EMDR® session I began to see that the nightmares were related to experiences I suffered at the hands of
a "loving female relative," Aunt Ruby. One of the first incidents I remembered was of her shoving me into the small,
dark, linen cabinet in the bathroom. She'd lock me in that
cramped little space from the outside and left me there for

hours. I was told that if I made any noise, I'd be left there even longer.

However, Laurel did not want to delve into this issue because I was still on shaky ground. I was struggling to stay sober and had only been on antidepressant medication for one month.

My nightmares were relentless, and I grew more agitated daily. Consequently, we were only able to postpone addressing the cabinet incidents in our EMDR® work for less than two months. That next EMDR® session revealed aspects of sexual abuse—inappropriate touching—and was the most terrifying session I'd had.

At this point, Laurel introduced me to the fact that it was the little girl inside me that was hurt and frightened. We needed to communicate with her and make her feel safe and protected as I relived those episodes. This was very important because many more incidents surfaced and my horror escalated.

I believe now that those incidents I'd repressed during my childhood were bursting forth because I was sober and felt safe with Laurel. The more sessions we had, the more my trust in her grew. She was very consistent. She never lied to me or got angry with me. She was patient and caring. If she didn't know the answer to a question I asked, she would admit she didn't know. And, she had such a strong belief in the EMDR® process and its ability to heal.

This was very important because my sessions into the past were trips to hell and back. My memories were so clear, so detailed. For example, in one session I was three years old again and could hear sounds such as approaching footsteps, smell a burning cigarette, and—worst of all, feel the pain of my small body being violated.

My trust in Laurel was also important because sometimes during an EMDR® session I got stuck in a memory and couldn't process through the abuse scene. Other times I felt caught in a timeless void—neither in the past or present. These were terrifying places for a two-, three-, or four-year-old child. But, Laurel always retrieved me. Sometimes her voice pulled me back to safety and at other times she stepped into the memory, held my hand, and led me back.

For instance, we began one EMDR® session by focusing on a nightmare I'd had the previous night. Soon, a scene appeared of Aunt Ruby and me, age three, in a bedroom. I was afraid and upset but couldn't tell Laurel what was happening. Thus, she couldn't help me in the memory. What she did do, however, was care for me by stopping the memory and calming me by taking me to my safe place.

In our next session, we worked on this bedroom incident and learned why the prior session had been so difficult for me: *my little girl had been told not to tell anyone.* Aunt Ruby had threatened her with severe punishment if she told anyone. Only because of my little girl's trust in Laurel could the child break her silence. The memory was excruciating; it was of being tied up naked and sexually abused with the sole purpose of causing the little girl extreme pain.

After this session, I thought that the worst was over. Again, I was wrong. The memories appeared in an order that went from least bad to the worst. But I persevered. I did not give up. I realized that I had two choices: I could either move forward and grow or I could remain the same and forfeit a peaceful and more rounded life. The former, however, would entail ups and downs, highs and lows, happiness and sadness, and pain and struggle.

I was able to continue from week to week and month to

month because I had powerful glimpses of my improvement. Actually, I was better than I'd ever been! Also, I found that once I'd processed an incident to completion with EMDR®, that incident never returned. Others emerged, but never the same one twice. I was greatly encouraged feeling I wouldn't remain in a vicious cycle: there was always an end. After I'd processed an incident to completion in session, I felt different. I felt light, as if a concrete brick had been removed from my body and pressure had been released. With this new freedom, I began doing things I'd never done before and had many insights.

For instance, one day I just had to get out of the house so I went for a drive in the country. I had never been on the road before and I suddenly became quite frightened that I would get lost. And then in the next moment the fear was gone, replaced with a feeling of supreme calm and the knowledge *that since I was heading toward no particular destination, it was not possible for me to become lost.* What is even more amazing about this experience is that the concept of no fear—no particular destination—began to develop into a life philosophy for me. Such insight had never happened to me before and I still feel awe when I remember this beautiful moment.

More haunting nightmares lead to another session of EMDR®, which again raised a memory of my lying naked on a bed, a belt tying my hands, and of being sexually violated. However, this memory was different: I was suddenly untied and forced to perform oral sex on Aunt Ruby.

My little girl had a big problem. She was afraid to tell Laurel what was happening because she feared that Laurel would think she was a bad girl and get mad and abandon her. But, Laurel explained to my little girl that she was good, that it was not her fault, that the adult was responsible, and that the adult was bad—very bad.

After such abuse scenes, I had trouble believing that what I'd just experienced was a memory of something that happened more than thirty years ago because while going back to the scene with Laurel, I relived the thoughts, emotions, and body sensations I'd had as a child. Often, after ending an EMDR® session, my back hurt, my wrists ached, and my mouth felt icky. I would feel sick, disgusted, repulsed, and angry. It took a long time for these feelings to go away.

Another particularly scary thing for me was that I felt as if I were a time bomb. Seemingly unrelated events in a movie, television program, or newspaper article would trigger my fear, agitation, and a series of nightmares. Laurel used these feelings and nightmares as starting points for our EMDR® sessions, and scenes of abuse would emerge. Eventually, I realized that I wasn't feeling freaked for no reason. There *was* a reason: my body was signaling me, and with EMDR® we would get to the reason and move through it.

MEMORIES OF "MY LOVING AUNT EMILY" SURFACE

I was processing a sexual abuse memory that featured Aunt Ruby when, suddenly, I became completely terrified. Actually, it was more of my sensing that Aunt Emily was there in the bedroom. Laurel and I had the same thought at the same time: "Was there someone else in the bedroom?" At that point, I didn't want to know the answer. I'd been through months of hell processing horrible incidents relating to Aunt Ruby, I was struggling to stay sober, and I felt incapable of handling any more shocking discoveries. I was emotionally and physically exhausted. So, we put off finding the answer. Finally, about six weeks later, the truth refused to wait any longer. I was in turmoil, suffering from bad dreams, interrupted sleep, agitation, depression, and headaches.

We scheduled an EMDR® session and returned to the original memory scene with Aunt Ruby. We had my little girl turn around, and she saw Aunt Emily standing in the doorway, watching, and awaiting her turn.

This revelation broke my heart because as a teenager and adult I'd deeply loved Aunt Emily. We had a strong and special connection, and such love does not occur often during one's lifetime. Finding out that she was also responsible for harming me created pure agony.

I wanted to remain in denial. I didn't want to look at the truth. I wanted these memories to disappear. But my attempts at denial caused tremendous turmoil between my adult self and my little girl. She knew the truth and wouldn't permit me to turn my back on it.

I compromised by stopping my outright expression of denial, but I didn't fully accept the truth either. For awhile I took some comfort in believing that Aunt Emily was just a follower of Aunt Ruby and just participated in what had been initiated by her—that Aunt Emily just wanted sexual satisfaction and was not mean. This belief was short-lived because each succeeding memory revealed the undeniable fact that Aunt Emily was just as brutal as Aunt Ruby. Aunt Emily was cruel, heartless, mean, deceitful, and devious. She lacked common decency and a moral code of ethics.

Seeing the truth and integrating this information were totally different issues. On one hand, I had a nice aunt with a nice face; on the other, I had a cruel and evil aunt with a mean face. I was a princess to one and a rag doll to the other. How could these faces belong to the same person?

I was deeply conflicted. I was grieving the loss of my once-beloved aunt, and at the same time I was angry at myself for grieving because she had betrayed me—a small, innocent child. I felt something was wrong with me because I felt such different emotions at the same time.

Thankfully, this prolonged agony ended when, during an EMDR® session, I realized that the Aunt Emily whom I supposedly loved had never actually existed. To trick me into trusting her she had acted like a nice person. *I realized she was like an actress playing different roles. The person I loved was the character she played—not who she was.* As a child, I didn't know that she was only acting: I believed she *was* the nice aunt. My confusion vanished, and I grieved the loss of my illusion of having had a loving aunt.

I realized the damage incurred by my aunts. I saw that I'd lacked trust in my ability to handle my life and lacked confidence in my judgment. I'd struggled with a never-ending and terrifying feeling of being without control—I'd navigated through days, months, and years on automatic pilot. I did what I'd always done because that was familiar and I knew what to expect. I'd not comprehended that these ways were harmful.

I also realized that I was disconnected from my physical self; I was unaware of basic needs: when to sleep, eat, or stop drinking,.and when to see a doctor. Also, I was absolutely unaware of my sexuality.

I distrusted other people and looked upon everyone I encountered as an enemy. I searched relentlessly for clues in words, gestures, and body language that would reveal the stranger's true nature—his or her true face. Meanwhile, I shielded myself by erecting invisible walls from any harm they might inflict on me.

MEMORIES OF UNCLE BILL: A "HAPPY-GO-LUCKY GUY" WHO LOVED CHILDREN

Besides my "loving aunts," I had a "loving uncle." Uncle Bill always seemed happy and easygoing, and he enjoyed company. He went to great lengths to make his young visitors feel welcome; although he had no young children of his own, he always had an abundance of toys, games, comic books, and candy. Yep, Uncle Bill was a real nice, happy-go-lucky guy.

Or so I'd thought. In therapy I learned otherwise. He was a pedophile with a definite strategy. Nothing at his house happened by accident. He was an expert at luring young children into his traps.

Although he differed from my aunts in his temperament, he was similar to them in that he used me—an innocent young child—to satisfy his sexual desires. He was different in that his attitude wasn't brutal. He seemed to believe that I liked what he was doing—that I was experiencing pleasure. It is difficult to understand this because he was into anal sex— an extremely painful act for a little kid.

I knew that my problem with trust as an adult stemmed from being abused as a young child by relatives. I had difficulty with trust—mostly, trusting myself. I doubted my ability to correctly judge whether the people I came into contact with were good or bad, nice or mean, or whether they meant to harm me. Consequently, I was isolating myself from new experiences and relationships. My trust in people had been destroyed.

Because I'd trusted my Uncle Bill, Laurel and I did an EMDR® session in which we targeted memories related to him because he definitely was not who he had appeared to be. Laurel suggested that the adult me observe what was taking place; Laurel thought that the adult would see and understand things that the child couldn't comprehend. My adult *did* see many things that alerted her that Uncle Bill was not to be trusted. She saw that the curtains were closed and the lights were dim. There was an incredible collection of toys, comic books, and candy. The doors were locked. My uncle was consuming alcohol and had an odd expression on his face. My adult self felt a chill pass through her entire body that caused her to pick up the little girl and run like hell out of that house.

The adult immediately questioned why a single man with no children would have a ton of toys and candy in his home. My questioning enabled my adult self to realize that he used these items to lure innocent, unsuspecting children into his lair.

Wow! What a session! I finally understood that I could scan my surroundings, analyze the available information, intuitively assess the situation, and act! Now I can trust myself and venture into the world.

Healing My Sexuality

In working with Laurel, I learned how impaired my ability to listen to my body's signals telling me that I was hungry, thirsty, tired, or ill was. I healed as we worked. But the most damaged area—and the hardest to write about—was my sexuality. I was uncomfortable talking about it. At first, I couldn't talk about it—I couldn't even look at Laurel. I just stared at the floor and refused to be drawn into discussion. Laurel suggested that I write my thoughts, and thus we began our work. Eventually, I could communicate verbally with her.

I had never recognized myself as being a sexual being. Rather, I had a body that merely accompanied my mind wherever it went. My body was a mass that could move or be still, stand, sit, or recline. I was completely disconnected from my sexuality because I'd been forced to participate in sexual behavior at too early an age. My child's confusion became my adult's.

Pleasure and pain repeatedly arose as themes in my sessions. As a child, I'd been touched in ways that gave me pleasure; then I would be touched in ways that caused great pain. I (the child) knew that what the adults were doing to me was bad— but sometimes it felt good. Therefore, I reasoned, my body must be bad to have felt good. I must be a very bad girl because I had a bad body.

In many EMDR® sessions, Laurel explained to the adult me and my child that everyone's body will experience pleasure when touched in certain ways, in certain areas, and that this is normal. The little girl's body had reacted in a normal way. She was a *good* girl with a *good* body. The adults were bad, very bad.

Integrating such new information involved two levels: both my child *and* adult needed to understand, and I worked hard; eventually, the reasons for my past choices and behaviors in my relationships with men dawned on me. This powerful knowledge showed me that all of my relationships revolved around the same pattern. I'd choose a guy who was a lot like me. He'd not be good at expressing feelings and wouldn't be interested in a deep, meaningful relationship because he didn't know what that meant. He'd be a loner. Most importantly, he'd be addicted to alcohol or drugs so that he wouldn't hassle me about my excessive drinking, and he'd be numb, as I was, when we were having sex.

Since identifying this underlying pattern and changing my attitude, I've shifted my values. I desire a relationship with a man who would lead a drug/alcohol-free life and be willing to express his feelings. Sexual intimacy would be based on mutual love and affection and he would desire a deep, spiritually-connected, "let's breathe the fresh air" type of relationship. What a change!

Who Am I?

During my recovery I asked, "Who am I?" This was very frightening for quite some time because the question was new to me. Other questions followed: Who am I in relation to myself? to my family? to nature? to the world in which I live? What am I doing with my life? Where am I headed? What is my purpose in being alive?

Time passed, and I experienced small bursts of wisdom and insight. I realized that discovering the answers to my questions was the beginning of my inner journey, my quest to wholeness. I realized, too, that as in any journey there will be times when I am frightened, but there will also be times of pure joy and peace and that I couldn't let fear control and immobilize me.

My Life Is Transformed

How has EMDR® changed my life? Well, the major change is that for the first time, I HAVE A LIFE. Before EMDR®, I just existed. I went through my daily routines on automatic pilot. My lonely existence was painful and joyless.

Now, however, I'M ALIVE! I'M FREE! I'M INDEPEN-DENT! I'M HAPPY! I feel connected to myself and to the world in a way that few people are. I'm one with myself on all levels: physically, emotionally, spiritually, and intuitively. I can contact my intuition and use it to guide my decisions, knowing that what I am doing is right and true for me. Because I can wait patiently for my wisdom to surface, I can remain calm. I experience little stress for I know that the answers will come.

My new ability to delve within myself amazes me—I'd certainly never been taught to look within for answers. Supposedly, the answers were in books, in schools, and in the words of experienced, intelligent people.

Somehow, my EMDR® work also encouraged me—unexpectedly—to explore my spirituality. Although I shied from this area at first, I discovered that spirituality is not the same as religion. Religion to me is rules and regulations, good or evil, and heaven or hell. Nothing in between is acceptable. I was taught to seek answers from priests, nuns, the Bible, or other "holy" literature. However, I found out that I can access my soul directly. I don't need a "middleman." Spirituality is an inner exploration, a lifelong journey of discovery.

My new connection with the world amazes me. I'm discovering many facets of it through all of my senses. It's so exciting! I *hear* birds singing and children laughing. When I commute to work, I *see* beautiful rainbows to which other drivers seem oblivious. I purposely stand in the rain so I can *feel* the drops touch my body.

Sobriety is no longer a challenge. I've absolutely no desire or need to drink alcohol; that terrible addiction no longer has a vise-like hold on me. My sobriety is a simple fact: I just don't drink alcohol anymore. Although I've read the "facts" regarding the lifelong potential for relapse, I don't foresee any problems.

Whereas my life prior to EMDR® work lacked direction, now I'm constantly headed forward. I'm not worried about tomorrow because I know that the actions and decisions that I make today will shape my future. I truly believe that I can handle whatever comes my way. My newfound confidence assures me that I can deal with the good and bad, happiness and pain, easy and difficult times.

Melanie's story beautifully illustrates how EMDR® can transform a life. Like the mythical phoenix who was consumed and transformed by fire and arose from the ashes to soar through the sky, Melanie and other EMDR® clients have gone directly into their pain, where it was burned away, and they emerged free from the past. Many of these clients feel reborn to themselves, fresh and alive, many for the first time.

Like so many of my other clients, Melanie experienced a life transformation that took her far beyond anything she had imagined possible. EMDR® work often exceeds recovery. I continue to be inspired by the transformations I see in clients for whom there had been little hope for change. The enthusiasm that I and my EMDR® colleagues have for this method has inspired a deep desire to bring this therapy out of the office to people everywhere who have experienced trauma. Compassion and a desire to help others is shared by thousands of EMDR® practitioners and, I believe, represents the "spirit" of EMDR®.

This spirit is not a belief or an ideal. Rather, it is a spontaneous heartfelt desire to help others who are suffering. We who are fortunate enough to have this marvelous tool to alleviate suffering feel blessed in the process of helping others. Facilitating another person's release from suffering brings such joy—and this joy naturally seeks extension to others.

This spirit is exemplified by the Vietnam War veteran EMDR® trainer Steven Silver, Ph.D., and other colleagues who risked their lives to go amidst gunfire into Zagrev and Sarajevo to train traumatized therapists in the EMDR® methodology so that they could help to relieve the terrible suffering in their countries. The newly-trained Croatian therapists requested that there be a training for the Serbs—their enemies!—in order to break the chain of violence and bring the possibility of a lasting peace. They recognized that violence begets violence and that the way to peace is through healing the trauma that violence has created.

We in EMDR®-HAP (EMDR® Humanitarian Assistance Program) see the potential to end the cycle of violence in the world. We share our humanity, and when the trauma and accompanying emotions are cleared, the desire for revenge vanishes. We also envision affecting future generations by breaking—with EMDR®—the chains of pain and halting its legacy. The adult who was sexually or physically abused who is treated with EMDR® therapy will not proceed to abuse his or her children.

When I look into the eyes of the EMDR® therapists who recount their stories of healing, I see love and hope. We have all been touched by something greater than we are. To facilitate the healing of great suffering is a tremendous gift *and* responsibility. Never before have we been able to help traumatized people so quickly and completely. Now, when I hear about someone who has been a victim of violence, I don't just feel sad—I feel hope that he or she can be helped and that his or her life does not necessarily have to be devastated.

Finally, EMDR® therapy can open us to the transpersonal realm. Objective forgiveness, profound love for self and others, trust in life, creative expansion, a deep sense of well-being and connectedness with all of life, spiritual insights and epiphanies, openings to the psychic realm, and experiences of transcendence and profound freedom are relatively commonplace for EMDR® clients. Consequently, clients often begin to ask larger life questions such as "Who am I?" "What is life?" and "What is death?" EMDR® processing clears obstructions, thus allowing us to contact our deepest truest selves. EMDR® processing often destroys the foundation of false constructs upon which clients have built their self-concepts, thus freeing clients to live more spontaneously and fully from a sense of wholeness. It is my desire that we continue to explore and expand the possibilities of EMDR® therapy as a method that goes beyond trauma recovery and opens us to our greatest potential.

APPENDIX A

How to Choose an
EMDR® Therapist

Successful EMDR® treatment depends upon the competence of the clinician. In the hands of a highly skillful, experienced therapist, EMDR® can be a power tool for healing.
However, the same tool in the hands of a less skillful or in-
competent therapist may not yield symptomatic relief—or
worse, may cause harm. Therefore, it is critically important
that you carefully interview your EMDR® therapist before deciding to work with him or her. Consider the following points
when choosing your therapist.

1. *The therapist should be an experienced and well-trained
clinician* because EMDR® therapy requires clinical expertise.
To be trained in EMDR®, the therapist must be either a licensed therapist or an intern who is currently being supervised
by an EMDR® Institute Level II trained clinician or the equivalent. The therapist you choose should also have experience
and training working with the problem for which you are
seeking treatment. For example, if you want to heal problems
related to childhood sexual abuse, you will want a clinician
with expertise in this area.

2. *Make sure your therapist has been properly trained in
EMDR®.* Many people claim to do "eye movement work" or

"rapid eye treatment." However, *to be an EMDR® therapist, one must have received EMDR® Level I and/or Level II training through the EMDR® Institute or have been trained in a graduate school or university course approved by EMDRIA (EMDR® International Association).* I have heard many accounts of people claiming to be trained in EMDR® when, in fact, their entire training consisted of watching the "20/20" television special on EMDR®, reading an article, or hearing a one-hour EMDR® presentation. A clinician who practices EMDR® without adequate training is *professionally unethical.* Unfortunately, irresponsible clinicians as well as nonclinicians all too often practice EMDR®.

As of this writing there has been no certification developed in EMDR®. However, the EMDR® Institute is currently developing a proficiency assessment procedure. Because no formal certification currently exists, *EMDR® training*—either from the Institute or from a graduate school or university course—*does not guarantee competence.* As a facilitator at dozens of EMDR® Institute trainings, I have seen many therapists leave the training without what I consider minimal competence for using EMDR®. Consequently, I highly recommend that you carefully interview your therapist.

3. *Has the therapist had advanced training—at a minimum, EMDR® Level II or its equivalent through a graduate school or university?* A clinician with Level I training is trained adequately to work with simple, straightforward problems such as single-incident trauma. This same clinician is not adequately trained to work with complicated childhood traumas and phobias. EMDR® Institute *trainers* and *facilitators* are the most highly-trained EMDR® practitioners.

4. *Has the therapist received consultation in EMDR® fol-*

lowing his or her training in EMDR®? This information informs you whether or not the therapist has continued to deepen his or her understanding and competence with EMDR® therapy.

5. *How much experience does the therapist have using EMDR®?* You will want to know how often he or she uses EMDR® and with what kinds of problems. How long has he or she been using EMDR®? What is his or her success rate with EMDR® therapy?

6. *The therapist's beliefs and attitudes play an important role in the success of EMDR®.* What are his or her beliefs about the potential healing of your particular problem? What are his or her beliefs about EMDR®'s usefulness? If he or she doesn't believe EMDR® can help you, you might want to look elsewhere. You might also ascertain his or her beliefs about healing. For example, a mother wishing to overcome her grief regarding the death of her child will be impeded in recovery if the therapist believes such a death "is something you never get over, and you'll have to suffer with it for the rest of your life."

7. *The therapeutic relationship is very important.* Can you trust this therapist to create a safe place for doing this deep work? Is he or she comfortable with your expressing intense emotion? Can you be yourself with him or her or do you feel you must behave in a certain way? Is the therapist compassionate? Could you develop a good rapport with this person? Does this therapist seem genuinely human? Do you feel this person maintains good "boundaries"?

8. *Has this therapist been an EMDR® client?* Has he or she experienced EMDR® as a genuine client—not simply in training exercises—so that he or she knows personally what it is like to dive into intense emotions and emerge?

APPENDIX B

Resources

Eye Movement Desensitization and Reprocessing International Association (EMDRIA)

>3900 East Camelback Road, Suite 200
>Phoenix, AZ 85018-2684
>(602) 912-5300; Fax (602) 957-4828

Nonprofit organization established for the continued professional and educational support and development of professionals trained in EMDR®. EMDRIA sponsors an international conference and specialty trainings, has a membership directory and referral services, and publishes a newsletter along with information on new articles on EMDR®. EMDRIA provides training standards for institutional training programs and certification of EMDR® trainers. In the future, it will publish a journal.

Eye Movement Desensitization and Reprocessing Institute (EMDR® Institute)

>PO Box 51010
>Pacific Grove, CA 93950-6010
>(408) 372-3900; Fax (408) 647-9881

Dr. Francine Shapiro is the founder and executive director of the EMDR® Institute, which provides Level I and Level II EMDR® trainings internationally to licensed therapists, as well as advanced clinical application workshops in areas such as sexual abuse, working with children, performance enhancement and substance abuse treatment. The Institute also provides an international referral service to EMDR® Institute-trained therapists.

EMDR® Humanitarian Assistance Program (EMDR®-HAP)

> EMDR®-HAP
> PO Box 1542
> El Grenada, CA 94018
> (415) 728-5609; Fax (415) 728-2246

Nonprofit service organization which provides pro bono training in EMDR® for mental health professionals in areas of great need such as where there has been a war or disaster. EMDR®-trained volunteers also provide treatment for individuals surviving recent traumatic events. In addition, EMDR®-HAP assists in developing EMDR® applications for new populations and supports research on EMDR®.

Index